Investing Worldwide III

February 23–25, 1992
Amelia Island, Florida

Sponsored by the
Association for
Investment Management
and Research
and the
International Society of
Financial Analysts

an *AIMR* publication

To obtain an AIMR Publications Catalog or to order additional copies of this publication, turn to page 78 or contact:

AIMR Publications Sales Department
P.O. Box 7947
Charlottesville, VA 22906
Telephone: 804/980-3647
Fax: 804/977-0350

The Association for Investment Management and Research comprises the Institute of Chartered Financial Analysts and the Financial Analysts Federation. The International Society of Financial Analysts is a society of the Financial Analysts Federation.

This publication is designed to provide accurate and authoritative information in regard to the subject matter covered. It is sold with the understanding that the publisher is not engaged in rendering legal, accounting, or other professional service. If legal advice or other expert assistance is required, the services of a competent professional should be sought.

From a Declaration of Principles jointly adopted by a Committee of the American Bar Association and a Committee of Publishers.

ISBN 1-879087-19-7

Printed in the United States of America

October 1992

Table of Contents

Foreword

Cultural differences have a distinct impact on client objectives and portfolio construction. Recognizing this, the Association for Investment Management and Research and the International Society of Financial Analysts selected cultural factors as the focus of the third *Investing Worldwide* conference.

This proved to be an appropriate choice, which is evident in the pages that follow. *Investing Worldwide III*, which includes a selection of presentations from the conference, contains unusually insightful analyses. Like 1990's *Investing Worldwide* and 1991's *Investing Worldwide II*, the 1992 conference gathered expert investment professionals to address varied aspects of international investing. These include geographical perspectives on opportunities in Europe and the Pacific Rim, advances in equity valuation models, and ways to build an international research team. Other speakers broached provocative topics of more general interest to investment managers. We hope you find all of their comments stimulating.

AIMR and ISFA wish to thank all those whose time and commitment contributed to the success of the meeting and ultimately to the substance of this publication. These include not only speakers but also attendees, whose contributions were both pertinent and enlightening. Special thanks are extended to Richard F. DeMong, CFA, who edited these proceedings and lent a keen and practiced eye to the publication effort. Also, Arnold S. Wood, president of ISFA, provided his usual wise counsel as chairman of the *Investing Worldwide III* conference; his leadership continues to spark enthusiasm for international concerns within the entire investment community.

A final note: In reading the contents of this publication, please keep in mind that *Investing Worldwide IV* will be held February 21–23, 1993, in Pasadena, California.

Katrina F. Sherrerd, CFA
Vice President
Publications and Research

Investing Worldwide III—An Overview

Richard F. DeMong, CFA
Professor of Commerce
Director, Center for Financial Services Studies
McIntire School of Commerce
University of Virginia

ncreased returns and decreased risks are two potential advantages of investing in non-U.S. markets. Several conditions make these results possible. For example, if non-U.S. money and capital markets have a greater growth potential than U.S. markets, returns are likely to be higher; if the U.S. dollar depreciates relative to other currencies, returns are likely to be higher; and if U.S. and non-U.S. markets are not highly correlated, overall portfolio risk is diminished. To a certain extent, all three of these conditions prevailed during the 1980s, and U.S. investors were able to gain a superior return with lower risks by investing outside North America.

The return advantages of overseas investment have been well documented. For example, Professors Eun, Kolodny, and Resnick found that, on a risk-adjusted basis, "The majority of international [mutual] funds outperformed the S&P 500 Index during the 10-year period of 1977–86."[1] The average annual compound return of the Europe/Australia/Far East Index from 1971 to 1991 was 14.3 percent, and the S&P 500 showed an 11.9 percent return.

Another reason for investors to allocate funds overseas is the simple fact that the majority of equity investment opportunities are outside the United States. Morgan Stanley Capital International estimates that the capitalization of U.S. stock markets represents only 40 percent of the total in stock markets of the major industrial countries.

Many stories have appeared in the press encouraging people to invest overseas. This advice has not gone unnoticed among fund managers. According to Davanzo and Kautz, U.S. pension funds now have $100 billion invested in international stocks and bonds.[2] They expect U.S. pension fund managers to increase their investment in overseas equities and fixed-income securities to $340 billion by the end of 1995.

A basic rule of investing is to understand the risks and potential returns of an investment before committing any funds. The presentations reproduced in this proceedings explore the impacts of culture, accounting traditions, currency exchange, and trading and custody management on the value of investments in nondomestic markets.

The Importance of Knowing Culture

Cheong correctly argues that failing to consider culture can be as serious as failing to use modern analytical tools. To Cheong, culture is one of the myriad factors that must be considered before investing internationally. As important as culture is to international investing decisions, it is often omitted from investment textbooks.

Cheong cites the following elements that are important to investment decisions: investment sophistication, flow of information, valuation perspectives, size and liquidity of the markets, political factors, and such local features as

[1]Cheol S. Eun, Richard Kolodny, and Bruce G. Resnick, "U.S.-based International Mutual Funds: A Performance Evaluation," *The Journal of Portfolio Management* (Spring 1991):93.

[2]Lawrence E. Davanzo and Leslie B. Kautz, "Toward a Global Pension Market," *The Journal of Portfolio Management* (Summer 1992):79.

national and local holidays and specific types of securities. Each component can significantly affect the valuation process and the short-term price of an asset. Cheong also points out that investors have their own culture biases, which may affect their investment decisions. This bias should be understood so that foreign investments can be based solely on relevant factors.

Cheong warns against placing too much emphasis on cultural factors, however, because in the long run, fundamental factors will be more decisive. For example, the Asian markets have done well because of the fundamental successes of their economies rather than cultural factors.

Howell agrees that, although cultural differences affect the way portfolio managers construct their portfolios, those differences are essentially determined by macroeconomic factors. He illustrates this point by noting that German investors prefer bonds and British investors prefer equities. These national preferences for certain types of securities reflect the inherent risk and return expectations within each market. Howell also points out that the percentage of institutional ownership of equities and the number of private pension funds in a country will affect the valuation of that country's assets.

Howell argues that liquidity is a key factor in explaining the price of an asset. As an example, he uses several liquidity ratios to predict the movements of the markets. He focuses on price–money and price–gross domestic product ratios, in which price refers to stock market capitalization and money refers to the broad money supply.

Bertocci suggests that the best way of knowing about and adjusting for cultural differences is to hire local staff. Like a manufacturing company, an investment firm must study the marketplace thoroughly and develop a system for gathering and analyzing appropriate information. The firm should use this information in the context of a consistent business strategy and stick to that strategy.

Accounting, Traditions, and Culture

According to Aldous, systems of accounting are also a reflection of culture. Aldous says that a country's accounting system develops on the basis of traditions within the country's economic system. He claims that the elaborate means the British developed to finance Britain's mercantile economy required accounting to aid the process. The French developed their system of accounting on the basis of codification of laws under Napoleon, and the Germans developed their accounting system based on the Prussian codification of Roman law.

Because these different accounting systems give distinctive forms and contexts to business in each country, analysts should understand the culture, language, and assumptions of domestic investors when they examine a set of accounting statements. A good analyst needs variable mental filters through which to analyze accounts on a comparable basis.

Some essential assumptions underlying an accounting system are attitudes toward value, authority, creditors, and audits. In addition, analysts must understand local governmental accounting regulations and definitions of such terms as "profit." Because accounting practices determine how revenue, depreciation, inventory expenses, pension expenses, capital expenses, currency translations, taxes, and bad debts are recognized, they will affect balance sheet values for current assets, including accounts receivable, inventory and securities, intangibles, and reserves. Analysts must also determine how much off-balance-sheet financing is allowed under a particular country's accounting principles.

Aldous says he hopes that the future will bring more standardization to the accounting practices of companies in different countries. He finds that inefficient information resulting from variations in practice leads to inefficient investment decisions and therefore to inefficient allocation of resources.

Geographical Considerations

Murphy says that culture is at the heart of the investment process and that geography provides significant insight into culture. Cultural history is the creation of a human geography—the patterns of language, religion, population distribution, industry concentrations, and human-induced environmental changes characterizing the world at any given moment. These cultural geographic factors fundamentally shape economic development. Superimposed on these cultural patterns are the political realities of different nationalities and ideologies. According to Murphy, an understanding of the cultural context is essential to assessing economic possibilities and prospects.

Latz emphasizes the importance of understanding the complex physical, cultural, and economic factors influencing attitudes toward and policies for national and regional development in the Pacific Rim. He finds the pace of change in the Pacific Rim slower than that in Europe. Also, the growth of Asian cities will require massive infrastructure investments in transportation, food production, communication, water supply, waste disposal, pollution control, and housing.

Latz argues that the bipolar world has given way to a multipolar world with new patterns of circulation of goods and services. These shifts will affect resource distribution, population growth, urban growth, regional growth, political structures, and economic institutions.

Economos describes an investment analysis in the Pacific Basin. He finds that the region's potential returns currently outweigh the potential risks. Economos cites the number of stock market opportunities, past stock market returns, high rates of economic growth, increasing regional prosperity, probusiness attitudes of the governments, and the region's Confucian ethic. Other reasons to invest in the region include its high levels of economic activity, increasing levels of foreign direct investment, rising living standards, and strong domestic demands. The disadvantages are slower global trade, changes in industrial composition, lack of infrastructure, shortage of skilled middle management, the historical emphasis on debt rather than equity capital, and political change.

Trading, Custody, and Currency Exchange Management

Rosenberg asserts that currency exchange management is an important, but distinct, aspect of international investing. Investment results can be either enhanced or undermined by the quality of currency exchange management. The currency decision should be made in conjunction with the market decision, the goal being to find the highest excess return after considering the currency outlook. Currency exposure can be managed by a unit within an investment firm, or this expertise can be acquired outside the firm. Regardless of how the currency exchange is managed, the firm should strive for the highest excess returns, not the highest absolute returns.

Trading and custody management are often overlooked in overseas investing, according to Kos, who finds that the costs of trading and custody management are critical to the investment process. He says trading costs generally are higher in non-U.S. markets, although they appear to be declining. Also, the average turnover of stocks within the aggregate markets has dropped during the past five years.

Currency exchange management can be more than a passive balancing of risks; it can evolve into an active allocation process based on expected exchange rate changes. The market offering the highest absolute return is not necessarily the market an investor should overweight. To determine which market to favor, a manager must consider the cost of hedging the currency exposure with forward or futures contracts. The market that should be overweighted is the market offering the greatest excess return relative to cash. Yield and yield curves are important factors to be considered in currency decisions, just as they are in investment decisions.

Advances in Equity Valuation

MacQueen notes that quantitative models have been more widely used in Europe during the past 10 years. European investors now generally accept the idea of using rigorous, systematic, disciplined investment management approaches rather than seat-of-the-pants management. They also have become more sophisticated in their ability to evaluate quantitative models—that is, to understand and test a model's definitions, methodologies, assumptions, inputs, underlying macroeconomic assumptions, economic rationale, range of validity, range of applicability, and the shape of the distribution curve.

Muller looks at two traditional quantitative models, value and momentum models. Value models use book values, yields, earnings, free cash flows, revenues, and dividends as inputs. The momentum models are based on technical analysis and include relative price momentum, relative earnings momentum, and trends in earnings estimates. More recent quantitative approaches to modeling use macroeconomic relationships or low-volatility strategies. Variables for these models may include interest rates, inflation, industrial production, and exchange rates. The purpose of these models is to aid investors in beating a benchmark return. The low-volatility models take a different track; they attempt to identify stocks with lower volatility or betas than the market average. These models also work in international markets.

Muller suggests investment managers should build their own models based on economic theory or identifiable patterns of market behavior. To do so, investment managers must keep their ears open for new ideas, test their models internally, quickly backtest a model over short periods, and be willing to take risks based on their models' results. Because models decay over time, however, managers must also be prepared to replace them when they no longer reflect current market behavior. Muller also identifies some of the hot topics in quantitative model building.

These presentations establish the importance of understanding the culture or context of international investment. They also emphasize the dynamic nature of business and investment climates overseas. What is true today may not be true tomorrow when global markets become a reality and when trading, accounting, and related regulations become more standard.

Cultural Impacts on Portfolio Construction

Henry Cheong
Chief Executive Officer
Worldsec International Ltd.

As managers expand investments into unfamiliar, less efficient, and less liquid markets outside the United States and Western Europe, they are certain to encounter regional or cultural differences. Although these and other local market insights are important, the fundamentals of financial analysis are more so.

Overseas diversification reduces risks and enhances returns. The practice of diversification, however, is not as simple as the theory. Returns from foreign stock markets can indeed be highly rewarding—witness the almost 400 percent increase in the Argentine stock market and the 41 percent increase in the Hong Kong stock market last year. Foreign stock markets can also be volatile, however—Japan during the past two years, for example. The question is this: To what extent are foreign markets driven by fundamental and technical factors, and to what extent are markets affected by cultural factors—those not normally found in investment textbooks?

Despite the maturity of the science of portfolio management, cultural factors do still matter. Failure to take account of them can be as damaging to performance as failure to use modern analytical tools. In the United States today, no fundamentally oriented fund manager ignores the insights to be had from technical analysis. No one simple solution to the problem of portfolio management exists, however. To improve the odds of winning, a manager must take into account a range of factors outside the traditional realm of investment research. Investment is as much an art as it is a science. The art lies in knowing when and when not to ignore cultural factors.

The art of investment management also lies in knowing how much investment technology to apply in the market under consideration.

Cultural Factors

As managers expand their investments from the known, well-researched, and liquid stock markets of the United States and Western Europe to unfamiliar, less efficient, and less liquid markets, they are certain to encounter regional or cultural differences. Many of these differences may be a matter of common sense, but they are ignored surprisingly often. These cultural factors include the following:

■ *Degree of investment sophistication.* In many markets, investors are still 5 to 10 years behind the more sophisticated U.S. and European fund managers. The importance of this gap cannot be overlooked. In investment matters, if investors are too far ahead, they are in fact behind.

■ *Information flows.* Accounting practices and disclosure rules vary greatly from country to country. In some countries, banks publish profits only after unspecified transfers to and from hidden inner reserves. The emphasis put on certain investment statistics also can vary significantly. For example, price–book-value ratio is a totally meaningless figure in Thailand, which taxes valuation surpluses regardless of whether they are realized. In

5

Hong Kong, annual valuation of investment property is mandatory, so a price-book-value ratio can be a useful figure.

■ *Differences in valuation perspective.* In many markets, the focus is more on earnings than on earnings per share. The momentum of earnings can be more important than the price–earnings ratio (P/E). In many markets, a cheap stock is one for which the unit price is low, and whether a warrant is cheap has nothing to do with the premium. Therein lies opportunity.

For example, a dividend discount approach to the valuation of the Cross Harbour Tunnel Company in Hong Kong, a franchise toll tunnel operator, is theoretically sound. The result, however, will bear no relation to the share price, which has consistently overvalued this company. Last November, a controlling, 24 percent block of shares in the company was sold at a 16 percent discount to the market price. This is a measure of the overvaluation.

■ *Size and liquidity of the market.* Most foreign markets lack the breadth and depth of the U.S. market. In some markets, a few companies can account for a large part of the market capitalization of the entire market or for a large part of daily market turnover. In many markets, individual investors are responsible for the bulk of turnover. In some countries, foreign ownership can be a sensitive political issue, and the percentage of a company that can be held by foreigners is limited. Cross-shareholdings may reflect political and strategic factors rather than purely investment considerations. Such cross-shareholdings reduce the free float and affect the liquidity of the stock in question. Small, illiquid markets can easily be disturbed by large flows of foreign funds.

Recently, foreign fund managers decided to be slightly less negative in their view of the Malaysian stock market. Sime Darby was aggressively bid up, partly because it was seen as a proxy for the entire market. The Jakarta Stock Exchange index rose from a low of 83 in 1988 to a high of 647 in 1990 as foreign investors flocked to participate in the deregulated market. The explosive performance of the market shown in **Figure 1** was attributable to a shortage of supply in the face of heavy demand from foreign fund managers. The question: Do the examples of the Sime Darby and the Jakarta stock market reflect cultural factors in Malaysia and Indonesia or cultural factors in London, New York, and other fund management centers?

Figure 1. Jakarta Stock Exchange Index, 1988–91

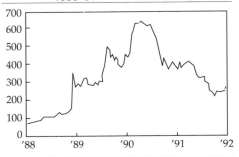

Source: Based on information from Jakarta Stock Exchange Index.

■ *Specific local factors.* As **Table 1** shows, the Hong Kong stock market has had 21 Chinese New Year rallies in the past 28 years. Is the regular seasonal Chinese New Year rally in some stock markets a specific cultural factor, or is it similar in principle to the "January" effect in the United States or the seasonality reflected in the adage "sell in May and go away"? Specific local market features may have short-term investment implications. In Japan, it pays to identify "ambulance stocks" early. These are stocks that are expected to outperform strongly. Brokers who have made a series of poor recommendations to a particular client would give him early notice of ambulance stocks to compensate him partially for his losses and to retain him as a client. In Hong Kong, it pays to identify "blue lantern stocks," which are the last stocks to participate in a rally and often signify an imminent short-term consolidation. Ignoring such factors is unwise.

Limitations of Cultural Factors

Clearly, given the complex factors affecting international diversification, in-

Table 1. The Complete Hang Seng Index Chinese New Year Form Sheet, 1964–91

Year	End of November	Year	End of February	Percent Change
1991	4,149.80	1992	4,727.95[a]	13.9%
1990	2,965.06	1991	3,552.14	19.8
1989	2,748.35	1990	2,951.98	7.4
1988	2,659.30	1989	3,012.68	13.3
1987	2,138.39	1988	2,418.08	13.1
1986	2,418.75	1987	2,877.87	19.0
1985	1,716.95	1986	1,695.30	−1.3
1984	1,128.10	1985	1,375.25	21.9
1983	852.90	1984	1,059.29	24.2
1982	704.03	1983	1,021.55	45.1
1981	1,450.22	1982	1,271.60	−12.3
1980	1,445.51	1981	1,487.88	2.9
1979	762.45	1980	914.91	20.0
1978	499.43	1979	526.87	5.5
1977	419.29	1978	413.03	−1.5
1976	400.77	1977	427.76	6.7
1975	313.52	1976	448.14	42.9
1974	174.85	1975	252.67	44.5
1973	514.71	1974	387.20	−24.8
1972	664.91	1973	1,625.63	144.5
1971	284.74	1972	342.79	20.4
1970	198.86	1971	209.16	5.2
1969	157.01	1970	174.06	10.9
1968	101.44	1969	115.39	13.8
1967	66.36	1968	64.46	−2.9
1966	81.25	1967	79.12	−2.6
1965	77.95	1966	85.81	10.1
1964	101.42	1965	98.08	−3.3

Number of UP years		21
Average change, UP years[b]		18.2%
Number of DOWN years		7
Average change, DOWN years		−6.9%

Source: Worldsec International Ltd.

[a]To February 10, 1991 only.
[b]Excludes 1972–73 and 1991–92.

vestors cannot rely solely on the disciplined application of modern investment technology. Nevertheless, investors should apply in foreign markets the analytical methods they use in the United States. Technical analysis is an essential starting point if they are to outperform. Local market insights are important, but fundamentals are more so.

Overemphasizing cultural factors is easy, particularly when market movements appear inexplicable. For example, the Japanese stock market is said to be impenetrable to outsiders, or at least not susceptible to the Western approach to investment analysis. During the 1980s, Japan became the most expensive market in the world and then briefly the largest. During this time, foreigners were surprised and bewildered by the strength of the market. Today, the obverse situation prevails, and the Japanese are bewildered by their market's weakness.

Cultural factors certainly influenced the trajectory of the boom and bust in Japan, but the rise and fall can be logically related to fundamentals. The Tokyo market began the 1980s at a premium rating of about 20 times earnings and a price–book-value ratio of a little over two times. These levels were justified by superior growth rates, different accounting policies, large corporate cross-shareholdings, and the rapid growth of Japanese savings. In the second part of the 1980s, however, the Japanese stock market soared to extraordinary valuation levels, suggesting it was subject to factors beyond the tools of Western analysts.

During the boom, getting close to a friendly Japanese broker and trying to understand the cultural differences were seen as the secrets of success. Japanese brokers were strong; the big four dominated the market. Individual investors accounted for the bulk of trading, and they could be influenced by aggressive salesmen to buy a particular "stock of the day" in the "theme of the week," whether it be export-related issues or hidden asset plays. To explain some of the gravity-defying stock performances, a lot of fuss was made about the alleged eccentricities of the Japanese market, which were supposed to stem from cultural differences. In the early 1980s, over-reliance on Western analytical tools and unwillingness to accept the dynamics of the market could have been counterproductive. The late 1980s was the time to ignore the domestic euphoria and focus instead on investment fundamentals, as understood in the United States and Europe. Knowing more about the local factors affecting a market can do no harm, but to suggest, as some did in Japan in the 1980s, that fundamental research is irrelevant is wrong.

The two most important factors responsible for the 1980s boom in the Japanese stock market were the increased involvement in equities by Japan's financial institutions at a time of rapid fund inflows and a long period of unusually low interest rates. The widely watched 10-year benchmark bond prices peaked in the spring of 1987 at a yield of only 4.2 percent, down from 9.7 percent at the beginning of the decade. The extended fall in interest rates laid the foundation for an extended period of asset inflation in equities.

The parallel with the situation in the

United States today is interesting. Despite a weak economic environment, Wall Street has performed strongly, buoyed by an extended fall in interest rates. If New York and Tokyo continue on their present trends, we will shortly see a situation in which the P/E of the Dow Jones Industrial Average exceeds the P/E of the first section of the Tokyo Stock Exchange (**Figure 2**). The comparison is somewhat distorted by the narrowness of the Dow's 30 constituent stocks and by the bad results for a few big U.S. companies, but the point is that nobody tries to analyze the performance of Wall Street by reference to U.S. culture.

Figure 2. Price–Earnings Ratios, Dow Jones Industrials and Tokyo Stock Exchange Section 1, 1990–91

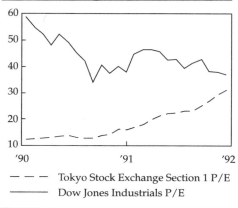

— — — Tokyo Stock Exchange Section 1 P/E
——— Dow Jones Industrials P/E

Source: Worldsec International Ltd.

As in the United States today, low and falling interest rates in Japan in the mid-1980s made the stock market attractive. Gradually, the expectation of appreciation in the stock market became self-fulfilling. All stock markets have a positive feedback loop, and this systemic feature is what caused the surprising boom in Japan in the late 1980s. The Hong Kong stock market also has this positive feedback characteristic. The foundations for an explosive performance in the Hong Kong stock market in anticipation of 1997 have already been laid, but nonetheless it will surprise investors when it occurs.

In Japan in the second half of the 1980s, a huge flow of funds went into equities and real estate. Tokkin funds (surplus funds from the insurance and corporate sectors, as well as from the banks, that are invested in equities) grew from $38 billion in March 1985 to $320 billion by the end of 1990. The equity weighting of the trust banks and pension funds, having been fairly flat during the early part of the 1980s, rose from a little more than 12 percent in 1985 to nearly 28 percent by 1989, and the size of their equity holdings grew by a factor of 10 times.

After the October 1987 stock market crash, the importance of Japan as an engine of world growth and an agent of stability in the world's financial system was reinforced. The official discount rate thus stayed at the record-low level of 2.5 percent until May 1989. The effect was to extend the magnitude and duration of the boom and to make the ensuing crash more pronounced than it otherwise would have been.

The liquidity-driven boom was led by the banking sector, which had profited from falling interest rates. Unfortunately, few foreign fund managers had bank shares, which were trading at extremely high P/E ratios. Furthermore, foreign investors were unaware that Japanese investors placed more emphasis on earnings growth momentum than on the P/E ratio. As a result, they underperformed. This underperformance could be considered as stemming from cultural differences, but what drove bank shares higher was the simple fundamental factor of strong earnings growth.

Asian Market Cultures

The collapse of the Japanese stock market is not a uniquely Japanese phenomenon. Excessive valuations and their subsequent deflation have been recorded in many markets. In 1973 and 1974, in Hong Kong, the Hang Seng index fell 90 percent in 21 months. More recently, the Taiwan Stock Exchange index rose from around 1,000 at the beginning of 1987 to a high of 12,495 in October 1990 before falling within eight months to below 2,600. It has since recovered to exceed 5,000. (Incidentally, Taiwan is a market worth considering.)

Extreme valuations do not occur only in countries that share a Confucian cultural heritage. In the United States, during the growth stock boom of 1961 and 1962, for example, IBM reached a P/E ratio exceeding 60 times. In another growth stock boom a decade later, "nifty fifty" stocks, such as Polaroid and Walt Disney, reached about 40 times and then fell for lack of earnings support. Booms and busts cut across national and cultural boundaries.

One reason culture features so highly in investor consciousness is the economic success of several Asian countries. The success first of Japan and then of the "dragon economies" is often attributed to the Confucian work ethic they share. It is true that people there work hard. This may indeed be attributable to cultural influences, but other explanations also apply. Without the social security systems that exist in the West, work equates to survival. Put bluntly, if people do not work, they starve. If they work hard, they can enjoy the good things in life. Asian workers are said to be culturally more docile and more productive. This may result from Confucian values, but the managers of Hyundai Motors might not agree that workers are docile. As far as productivity is concerned, some of the superior productivity of Asian workers may be an accounting phenomenon. Rather than working five days a week, if factory workers in the United States were to work six days a week as they do in Asia, plant productivity will automatically improve 20 percent. Overhead cost per unit of production would fall by about 17 percent. The beneficial impact on margins would be far greater. With increased profits, companies would be in a stronger position to reinvest for growth. The Confucian culture respects authority, and this can be conducive to good employee relationships and hence improved profitability. Management–employee relationships, productivity, and profitability are fundamental factors in the investment equation, but fund managers can consider the impact of Confucian culture on these factors only in a diffused, general manner.

A number of seemingly frivolous factors sometimes have a marked impact on Asian markets. In many countries, for example, astrology—the influence of the stars—is taken seriously. Fung Shui experts are consulted on every aspect of life: home, office, selection of a spouse or a business partner, and of course, the investment outlook. Fortune-tellers have been influential in such markets as Taiwan and Thailand, where individual participation in the stock markets is substantial.

Markets with a large retail interest spawn "crocodiles"—large private investors with extensive retail followings whose stock market activity is well publicized after the fact. These investors, and the punters who follow them, can have a major impact on share prices. Because publicity is essential for a successful ramp, foreign fund managers can easily keep abreast of developments by reading local newspapers. The more successful crocodiles tend to ramp shares with attractive fundamentals, which make the job easier, so do not be too proud to follow the crowd. The trick is knowing when to follow and when not to. Big crocodiles are particularly evident in bull markets, in which the common cultural attribute is greed. Speculative activity is always lubricated by a generous dose of rumor. Short-term fads can become self-feeding. In such a situation, think twice about selling an expensive stock. If the momentum is there, the stock will just get more expensive. Momentum trading, of course, cuts across cultural and national boundaries, and some investors in the U.S. stock market have even programmed their computers to take advantage of it.

In markets with significant retail participation, the absolute price of a stock is important. Of the 51 new listings in Hong Kong last year, 45 were priced at an "affordably" cheap price of around HK$1 a share. Such perceptions are important even in the United States, except that "penny stocks" have a negative connotation. In other words, in U.S. culture, "cheap" is not "value." Cheap may or may not represent value, and only research can tell.

Fundamentally, bonus issues should not be an important investment-deter-

mining factor. To argue that they should make no difference is too simplistic, however, because in an efficient market, the share price adjusts for the bonus issue. Share prices do not always adjust to the theoretical ex-bonus price. About 11 or 12 years ago, to avoid having shares locked up for registration, I sold Unicharm, a Japanese stock, just before it went ex-dividend and ex a 60 percent gratis issue. The unit share price went up on the ex-day—an effective one-day appreciation of more than 60 percent.

Political Factors

In diversifying overseas, investors should add an understanding of cultural factors to their bag of analytical tools. They also should develop an appreciation of local politics. In some overseas stock markets, politics can be a permanent factor on the investment scene. In other markets, it becomes important for a period of time (just before a general election, for example) before becoming dormant again. In still others, it is never dominant but is always close to the surface. Political risk is complex, generally with strong cultural overtones. Because of the colonial administration, investors in Hong Kong have never contended with a regular election timetable affecting the stock market. The 1997 handover to China, however, has pervaded the investment scene for about 10 years. The perceived political risk has been a long-standing negative. Yet on purely fundamental grounds, using simple analytical tools, the current strength in the Hong Kong stock market can be forecasted.

In October 1990, in the middle of the Gulf crisis, one analyst published four forecasts for the Hang Seng Index.[1] The four forecasts were related to four valuation benchmarks—gross domestic product growth, historic P/E, historic yield, and the world average P/E. The forecasts were 5,200, 4,150, 3,770, and 4,380, respectively, at a time when the

---

[1]Carlton Poon, *Hostages to Fortune: Various Hang Seng Index Forecasts* 3d ed. (London: Touchstone, 1990).

index was only 2,761. By February 1992, the index was over 4,700, a gain of more than 70 percent in 15 months. The point is that although local market factors—whether cultural, political, or other—can affect the short-term performance of a stock market, the market will sooner or later reflect fundamentals as understood in the West.

Investment prejudices reflect more on those that hold them than on those affected by them. Those who ignored Latin America because of its mañana philosophy are aware now of the cost of prejudice. A prejudice that Asia is a casino also still exists. This may have been true 10 or 15 years ago, but at least in Hong Kong, it is no longer true. The Hong Kong private investor has been so shelled-shocked by the October 1987, October 1988, June 1989, August 1990, and August 1991 events that he is probably one of the most conservative investors anywhere today.

Conclusion

Foreign markets are affected by fundamental and nonfundamental factors. The key parameters of investment are the same as in the United States. In the less-developed markets, however, the nonfundamental factors can sometimes have a greater impact than they generally do in the United States. This means that investors should approach each market with an open mind and be prepared to be flexible.

They should not, however, abandon the analytical tools they use in their domestic markets. Remember that you are not likely to be the first to hear foreign market rumors. Try to add value by bringing a longer term and global perspective to markets that tend to be local and short-term. These markets can be driven more by fear and greed than by investment fundamentals, just as in the U.S. market. As the American poet Henry Wadsworth Longfellow said, "Every human heart is human." Fear and greed are universal emotions that cut across all cultural barriers. When they temporarily dominate, rely more on fundamental analysis of value, and be patient. Investment overseas is difficult, but no more difficult than investment in the United States.

Culture and Portfolio Mix—Why Brits Prefer Equities and Germans Prefer *Bunds*

Michael Howell
Head of Global Strategy
Baring Securities Ltd.

National preferences for specific portfolio mixes are determined by macroeconomic factors. Local investors respond to differences in national fundamentals and to domestic taxes and other investment restrictions. Such cultural biases change over time, as do the macroeconomic influences that determine them.

The risk-averse German; the inscrutable Japanese; the phlegmatic, globe-trotting Brit; and the value-searching American—these are stereotypes of different national investors made by a notional global plan sponsor. How have these images arisen? And do the asset allocations of investors from different countries defy logic and simply reflect cultural influences?

Behind these stereotypes lie widely different approaches to asset allocation. As **Figure 1** shows, German investors prefer bonds; U.S. and U.K. investors prefer stocks, with U.K. managers especially favoring foreign equities; and Japanese investors cannot make up their minds.

Despite some commentators' prejudices, nothing in the physical or emotional makeup of the Continentals makes them any less risk averse than other countries. In fact, a glance at financial history shows that continental Europe has participated in more than its fair share of speculative investment booms and busts, lured by the scent of quick profit. Remember the Dutch Tulip mania and the Mississippi Bubble.

National portfolio mixes are mainly determined by macroeconomic factors. The fact that Germans favor bonds and Brits equities is not a fad; rather it is a rational response by local investors to differences in national fundamentals and to domestic taxes and other investment restrictions. Such cultural biases are not set in stone. The macroeconomic influences that determine them change over time.

Demands for different financial assets give rise to specialized financial intermediaries. Nonbank financial institutions, such as pension, life insurance, and mutual funds, have become commonplace in many economies. Like portfolio structure, the extent of this financial maturity varies among countries.

The Liquidity Model

Because financial markets are driven primarily by liquidity factors, different asset structures have important implications for investment returns. Today's wide range of performance returns at the macro or market level can be explained by aggregate valuation shifts. These valuation shifts mainly arise from changes in desired asset structures and the resulting flows of funds.

Such flips in the private or public sector's flow of investment dollars may be triggered by structural changes in savings behavior caused by, say, demographics or by cyclical forces generated by, say, desynchronized political or business developments among nations. In short, stocks and shares float on a sea

12

Figure 1. Portfolio Mixes—United States, United Kingdom, Germany, and Japan, 1990–91

United States (Pension Funds)

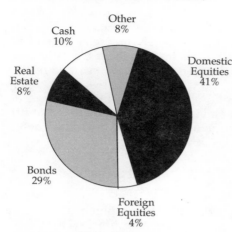

Other 8%
Cash 10%
Real Estate 8%
Bonds 29%
Foreign Equities 4%
Domestic Equities 41%

United Kingdom (Pension Funds)

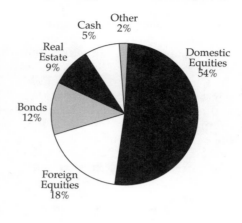

Cash 5%
Other 2%
Real Estate 9%
Bonds 12%
Foreign Equities 18%
Domestic Equities 54%

Germany (Insurance and Mutual Funds)

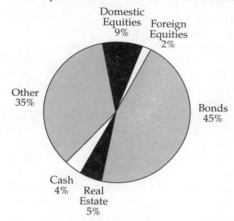

Domestic Equities 9%
Foreign Equities 2%
Other 35%
Cash 4%
Real Estate 5%
Bonds 45%

Japan (Life Insurance)

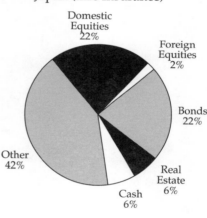

Domestic Equities 22%
Foreign Equities 2%
Other 42%
Cash 6%
Real Estate 6%
Bonds 22%

Source: Baring Securities Ltd.

of liquidity, with tides controlled by macroeconomic and institutional developments. We can only guess the timing and direction of the tides.

Rigid differences in national portfolio patterns emphasize why a "top-down" strategy of macroinvesting (the country-mix and asset-mix decisions) can consistently generate excess returns for many global investors. Other investors are limited in their investment choices, either formally (by regulations) or informally (by the local business climate, institutional background, and demographic pressures).

Existing moves toward financial deregulation and macroeconomic policy cooperation among the G-7 nations will help level the playing field and foster greater convergence of asset structures. Yet in the absence of a Big Bang, this convergence is likely to unfold slowly.

Meanwhile, national portfolio mixes will continue to differ markedly. This is fortunate for us as investors for two reasons: (1) Relative security returns will be greater because many investors will remain excluded from the global "honey pot," and (2) the relative stability of underlying asset allocations will allow the construction of a series of valuation benchmarks that can also gauge potential future returns.

We term these valuation benchmarks for equities price–money ratios (P/Ms), defined as the ratio between stock market capitalization and aggregate broad money supply by country. They can be used in a similar way to conventional price–earnings ratios (P/Es) to monitor value. Our analysis shows, however, that P/Ms are generally better predictors of future stock market returns than P/Es.

As **Figure 2** demonstrates, the P/Ms suggest that world stock markets are as cheap now as they have been on only four previous occasions since 1987. Moreover, in contrast to P/E multiples, they have not signaled an overvalued U.S. stock market in the past 12 months.

Figure 2. Global Price–Money Ratio and World Share Price Index, 1978–91

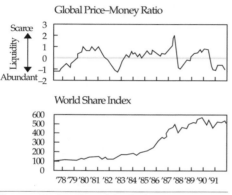

Source: Baring Securities Ltd.

Using the P/M framework, changes in share prices can be broken down into two broad components: a macrovaluation factor (the P/M itself) and a money or liquidity factor (M). The macrovaluation factor, or P/M, can be further decomposed into four elements: monetary velocity (GDP/M), institutional asset ratios (IA/GDP), institutional equity weightings (IE/IA), and relative institutional activity (inverted P/IE). Thus,

$$P/M = GDP/M \times IA/GDP \times IE/IA \times P/IE,$$

where

P	=	stock market capitalization,
M	=	broad money supply,
IA	=	value of nonbank institutional assets,
GDP	=	national income, and
IE	=	value of domestic equities held by domestic institutions.

Exhaustive work has been done by monetary economists to prove that monetary velocity (GDP/M) is stable and predictable over the medium term. The focus of this presentation, therefore, is on the other three elements of the equation: institutional asset ratio, institutional equity weightings, and relative institutional activity. Institutional portfolio structure, the first of these, depends upon an economy's liability structure and on the associated definition of risk.

What is Risk?

Investment decisions aim to maximize the risk-adjusted surplus between assets and liabilities over time. What exactly constitutes risk will influence this decision process. In a riskless or uniform-risk world, where investors have equal access to information and form their views in similar ways, asset structures should theoretically converge toward a common international pattern.

In fact, at the macro level, information flows are relatively homogeneous and decision making follows similar lines among global investors. Therefore, risk management is the paramount variable that, in practice, explains long-term differences in international asset structures. Risk is normally defined by the probability that the value of assets will fall below the value of liabilities at any time. Thus, risk is minimized when assets and liabilities move closely together. The tighter the string tying assets and liabilities the better.

The Role of Financial Assets

Because the asset allocation decision depends upon the liability mix each investor faces, portfolio mixes will differ in part because liability mixes themselves differ. *Bund*-oriented German investors may not necessarily expect absolute returns on bonds to exceed those on equities, but they should expect greater risk-adjusted bond returns. (Again, risk is defined relative to future liabilities.)

Two key determinants of long-term national liabilities are population maturity (pensions) and industrial maturity.

An aging population tends to demand longer duration financial assets, and a maturing economy tends to supply them. As economies mature, more roundabout ways of producing a profit will develop, tying up funds in capital-intensive projects, often for long periods of time. U.S. economist Raymond Goldsmith showed that the ratio between tangible and financial assets within an economy is directly related to its stage of economic maturity.[1]

A growing economy accumulates tangible assets such as plant, equipment, vehicles, and buildings. Markets that facilitate the transfer of these tangible assets between applications are termed capital markets. The divorce of ownership from the use of these assets gives rise to markets in paper claims, which are called financial markets. Economic efficiency should be directly related to the development of financial markets.

As economies mature, the mix of national portfolios between tangible and financial assets approaches stability. In our notation, (M + IA)/GDP becomes constant with a value of about 2. Therefore, changes in money will be directly offset by compensating changes in institutional asset holdings, assuming little change in GDP. In short, money and financial assets become near-perfect substitutes in a mature economy.

Goldsmith found that in more advanced stages of economic maturity, the relationship between money and other financial assets (M/IA) also stabilized. Consequently, changes in the amount of money in circulation are matched by changes in the holdings of other financial assets. Increases in the money supply should therefore lead to rising levels of equity and bond investment, much as the P/M model suggests.

The precise mix of these assets will depend both on prospective returns and on the assets' ability to minimize risk, which we have defined as the inability to match movements in liabilities. An economy's pension and demographic structures are important determinants of both the absolute size and the character of future liabilities.

----

[1]Raymond W. Goldsmith, "Corporate National Balance Sheets—A Study of 16 Countries, 1688–1978," 1985.

Privately Funded Pensions

The type of pension system (fully funded or pay-as-you-go) and the nature of the pension contract (final-salary based or fixed sum) affects the amount and character of the assets held. Equities match pension liabilities based on final salaries more reliably than bonds do, because future corporate dividend growth is likely to move broadly in line with wage and salary inflation. At the other extreme, bonds can match exactly the liabilities arising from a guaranteed future lump-sum cash pension.

The relative popularity of final-salary compared to fixed-sum pension schemes will be mainly affected by the outlook for inflation. In the United Kingdom, where domestic prices since 1960 have risen 4.6 times faster than those in Germany, a fixed future sum in current cash is less attractive than final-salary arrangements. Moreover, because a high underlying inflation rate has often been associated with significant year-to-year inflation volatility, the fixed sum's real value not only is less but also is more uncertain.

Thus, if a country's future liability structure is open ended and linked to the uncertain value of future wages and salaries, then the optimal asset structure that matches these liabilities will be skewed heavily toward equities. Using the previous notation, the IE/IA ratio will be relatively high.

Nonetheless, booming equity markets during the past decade have greatly benefitted investors in equity schemes over those who plumped for bonds. Competitive pressures among fund managers and the aggressive marketing of performance data are likely to encourage many new investors to favor equity schemes.

Some portion of equity funds may be invested in foreign shares, particularly if the home economy is relatively open to foreign trade. As future consumption expenditures will involve the purchase of foreign goods, the international purchasing power of a future pension stream can be maintained by holding foreign assets. This concept is termed "openness matching" and directly relates foreign asset exposure to an economy's import share.

Existing national asset structures not only show relatively low equity investment, they also reveal a limited exposure to international assets. According to the "openness matching" theory, this exposure is in general suboptimal. Optimal foreign holdings should average between 15 and 20 percent, compared with existing levels of 7.6 percent. Therefore, cross-border equity investment flows should increase alongside domestic equity holding. Already one share in five traded globally is either a foreign share or traded on a foreign exchange. By the end of the decade, this share could be one in three.

workers. In contrast, an aging population will put an increasing pension burden on the current income of young workers. To avoid this problem, pension financing can be brought forward in time through funding so that each successive generation pays for its own pensions. Under fully funded schemes, future benefits are directly linked to the final value of accumulated contributions.

The prospective aging of populations in several industrialized countries is illustrated in **Table 1**. The generous state welfare systems several countries adopted after World War II may have to be progressively pruned in the face of the burden arising from rapidly aging populations.

Table 1. **Aging Demographics, Selected Countries, 1950–2020**
(population older than 65 as a percent of total)

Country	1950	1980	1990E	2000E	2020E
United States	8.2	11.3	12.2	12.1	16.2
United Kingdom	10.7	14.9	15.1	14.5	16.3
Japan	5.2	7.8	11.4	15.2	20.9
Germany (West)	9.3	15.7	15.5	17.1	21.7
France	11.3	14.0	13.8	15.3	19.5
Switzerland	9.6	13.9	14.8	16.8	24.5
The Netherlands	7.7	11.5	12.7	13.5	18.9
Italy	8.0	13.5	13.8	15.3	19.4

Source: Organization for Economic Cooperation and Development.

Note: E = estimate.

Viewed globally, greater cross-border investing will lead to a reduction in local institutions' domestic equity holdings (IE) and an increase in their foreign equity holdings (part of P). Using the previous notation, the domestic institutional activity ratio (IE/P) will fall as local investors are crowded out by foreigners.

Demographics: Funded or Unfunded Pension Schemes?

The type of pension funding a country adopts may be influenced by demographic factors. A nation characterized by a rising young adult population and few retirees is likely to be able to fund these pensions easily from the swelling pool of contributions made by younger

If the pool of future workers is going to be significantly smaller than that of retirees, the prospects for unfunded or pay-as-you-go pension schemes are bleak. This problem is particularly acute in continental Europe. **Table 2** shows the distribution of assets among institutions in major European countries. Although the major European countries combined have more than U.S.$3 billion of directly funded pension fund assets, by far the bulk of these are held in the United Kingdom and The Netherlands. Consequently, several European governments are constructing a second tier of old-age provisions either directly through fiscal incentives or indirectly by liberalizing investment markets and investing institutions.

Consider, for example, the French

Table 2. Institutional Domestic and Foreign Equity Investment, Selected Countries, Year-End 1989
(billions of U.S. dollars)

Country	Pension Funds	Insurance Companies	Private Banks & Mutual Funds	Total Equities	Total Assets
France	—	59.8	24.6	84.4	437.3
Germany (West)	20.5	17.5	22.9	60.9	520.5
Italy	—	6.6	12.6	19.3	99.0
The Netherlands	23.3	8.9	11.6	43.8	284.4
Switzerland	7.3	0.8	214.0	222.1	884.9
United Kingdom	272.7	160.6	100.2	533.5	904.2
Total	323.8	254.1	385.9	963.8	3,129.2

Source: Baring Securities Ltd.

sociétés d'investissement à capital variable (SICAVs) and the United Kingdom's Personal Equity Plans and Additional Voluntary Contribution "top-up" schemes, all of which are similar to the U.S. individual retirement accounts. In Germany, the tax-advantaged *spezialfonds* have gained a new lease on life as pension vehicles. Nearly 1,800 funds are in operation, and inflows are running at the equivalent of U.S.$15 billion a year. Spain also recently liberalized its investment rules. The 1992 Spanish income tax law declared several asset classes exempt from capital gains tax. This has spurred strong growth in new pension assets and, particularly, in the more liquid unit trusts (closed-end mutual funds). In the nine months ending September 30, 1992, Spanish pension fund assets grew by 21 percent and unit trust funds rocketed by nearly 125 percent to Pta 2.71 trillion (U.S.$27 billion).

Mutual funds should not be forgotten, because they are already widely popular and may well become a major vehicle for pension investment in continental Europe. The French and Italian mutual fund industries enjoyed staggering growth during the 1980s, and within that decade, each virtually matched in size the assets the U.K. unit trust industry had taken since 1935 to accumulate.

Institutional and Regulatory Constraints

Prospective investment returns and asset structures are affected by differ- ences in taxation, regulation, and capital controls. German insurance companies are limited in their ability to invest in nondeutsche mark assets and cannot invest more than 20 percent of their assets in equities. Algemeen Burgelijk Pensioenfonds, the giant Dutch public sector pension fund, can only invest 5 percent of its assets abroad. In Greece, virtually all pension assets must be invested in government bonds, and Belgium and France have slightly less-strict requirements of 15 percent and 34 percent, respectively.

These controls are linked to prudence and to domestic macroeconomic needs. They have resulted in domestic equity holdings in continental Europe that average a meager 13 percent of total assets. For example, the current pension structure in Germany, where some U.S.$100 billion is held on corporate balance sheets, grew up as a prudential response to the hyperinflation in the 1920s. The "book reserve" method of self-investment by German companies, backed by state guarantee against bankruptcy, aimed to preserve the real value of assets. In a post-World War II world characterized by low German inflation, this system served German pensioners poorly. Investment decisions were not made in favor of the highest returns. Funds were simply provisioned against future pensions and then redeployed back into businesses, ensuring that German companies enjoyed low-cost capital.

This desire for low-cost capital is a

more general reason many investment restrictions still apply. By trapping funds within the local economy through, say, exchange controls, governments can reduce investment costs for domestic industry. The result may be a relatively high IE/IA ratio. More specifically, high-spending governments may wish to reduce their own interest costs by forcing investors to buy government bonds.

Government privatization policies also affect the private sector's asset structure. Generous discounts and easy payment terms on newly issued shares of former state enterprises would en-

extensive cross-shareholdings by industrial companies will boost overall stock market capitalization but will limit institutional participation. Under these conditions, the IE/P ratio will also slip.

Conclusion

Using the P/M framework illustrated in **Table 3**, with its implied emphasis on liquidity influences and flow of funds, differing national asset structures can be seen to depend on the role of institutions within the economy and the freedom these institutions have to manage their particular risks.

Table 3. Price–Money Ratios, Selected Countries, 1990

| Country | P/M | Billions of U.S. Dollars | |
		Stock Market Capitalization (P)	Money Supply[a] (M)
The Netherlands	1.05	148.6	141.1
United Kingdom	0.94	858.2	914.1
Japan	0.76	2,821.7	3,736.4
United States	0.75	3,095.4	4,123.3
Australia	0.68	107.3	158.1
Germany	0.54	355.3	660.8
France	0.31	304.4	982.4
Spain	0.31	111.4	359.3

Sources: Organization for Economic Cooperation and Development; Fédération Internationale Des Bourses De Valeurs.

[a]Money supply data refer to a broad aggregate, equivalent to M3 or M4.

courage higher investment in equities from institutions and retail investors. Although extensive privatization has already occurred in the United Kingdom, France, and Spain, considerable opportunity for privatization still exists in Europe. The United Kingdom has proposed the sell-off of its state railway and coal mining industries; the Bundespost is likely to be privatized in Germany; and in France, substantial state shareholdings still exist in key companies such as Credit Lyonnais, Banque Nationale de Paris, Elf-Aquitaine, and Union des Assurances de Paris. Using the previous notation, greater purchase of privatization issues by retail investors will push down the IE/P ratio by diluting domestic institutional activity.

Similarly, an antitakeover market or

A high P/M ratio is typically associated with a highly institutionalized economy, such as in the United Kingdom, United States, and Japan, with few constraints on equity investment. Security flows focus on pension, mutual, and life insurance funds, with a more limited role for banks. Investment guidelines are typically provided by trustees rather than by statutes.

A low P/M ratio, as in Germany, Spain, and France, typically depicts an economy with few investing institutions or with formal or informal constraints on equity investment. Banks often play a much greater role in these countries, and most investment guidelines are statutory.

These bank-driven stock markets are the norm in continental Europe. There, excluding Switzerland, the IE/P ratio is particularly low (institutions own only 16 percent of shares, compared to a 38 percent global average). Reinforcing this tendency are the Continent's relatively low IA/GDP (65 percent compared to a global 97 percent) and IE/IA ratios (15 percent compared to a global 29 percent). Share ownership is widespread in many European countries, but most shares are controlled by banks, either directly as long-term investments or indirectly as custodians of bearer shares.

Penal rates of taxation and the social upheavals that swept through Europe around the world wars encouraged the popularity of bearer shares. The legal postscript of many Continental companies, such as NV (Naamioze Venootschap) in The Netherlands and SA (Societe Anonyme) in France and Belgium, which reflect companies without named owners, is testimony to these events. Bearer shares have fostered the power of the banks as alternative providers of new capital, which is more often granted as loans. As the power of the banks has increased, so has their power to influence corporate policy and accounting techniques. The prudent, highly provisioned accounts submitted by German (and also Japanese) companies clearly have the imprint of the bankers' influence.

The bank-driven stock market model is fast becoming anachronistic. Aging populations, increased funds flow into pension and life insurance funds, deregulation, and greater macroeconomic policy coordination will push national asset holdings closer to a common structure. This structure is likely to be similar to the institutionally dominated Anglo-Saxon markets. Fund managers will be more interested in performance and profit and loss statements and less inclined to focus on book reserves and hence on balance sheet strength. If performance is the key future criterion of the emerging Continental equity fund managers, could they closely follow the Anglo-Saxon model and even throw Daimler-Benz, Commerzbank, or VEBA into the takeover ring?

These macroeconomic shifts will jolt portfolio patterns. Cultural stereotypes may be redundant by the end of the decade. Already, change is under way. Within the past few years, Japanese managers, spurred by demographic pressures and huge accumulated trade surpluses, have built up massive investments in high-yielding foreign securities. Since the start of the 1990s, U.S. and Continental funds, which average between 3 and 4 percent exposure in foreign assets, have been the most active cross-border investors. The Anglo-Saxon economies also are not immune to change. Their relatively mature pension structures are likely to force a progressive shift toward higher yielding assets as cash inflows become depleted by pension outflows. Bonds may soon replace equities. Slowly but surely, culture is changing.

Knowing the Client—The Impact Of Cultural Differences

Bruno Bertocci
Managing Director
Rockefeller & Co., Inc.

In Southeast Asia, the role of a regional office is to focus on clients and to build a commercial intelligence system for gathering marketplace data. Creating a successful office requires building a long-term, consistent business strategy; sticking to it; and using local people to modify and execute the strategy.

Cultural differences influence the investment process in many ways. Thus, knowing clients and their environment is very important. I will discuss the role of regional offices in marketing and the client environment in Southeast Asia—that is, Asia excluding Japan.

Regional Offices

The role of a regional office is twofold: to focus on clients in the marketing effort and to build a commercial intelligence system for gathering data about the marketplace—trends, competitors, and clients.

A well-planned staffing strategy is critical to the success of a regional office—particularly for marketing. One key to a successful staffing strategy is to hire local people who can rise to the top. A problem with regional offices is that companies tend to rely on expatriates to carry the company's culture abroad. The expatriate's role is to nurture local staff rather than represent headquarters. Many regional offices fail because the expatriate heading an office is a colonial overseer. I have witnessed this in U.S., French, and German companies. The expatriate sat at the top of the pyramid and did not help the local staff. Local staff people must have defined career paths and the potential to manage the branch. They also must have power and credibility within the organization; if they do not, the company is not likely to retain them, and the staff will not be effectively involved in the company's decision-making process or in implementing a successful marketing strategy.

The primary reason for having a local staff is to provide knowledge about the native area. To maximize this benefit, companies should hire the best people possible and then make staying with the company attractive. They must be given a real voice in marketing strategy; otherwise, the company will have some very expensive local personnel who are not involved in making good decisions.

A marketing strategy should be developed by both the regional office and headquarters, but the regional office is primarily responsible for executing the strategy. Headquarters should not second-guess the local staff. It should not alter an agreed-upon plan. The company should set goals and objectives, monitor progress, and avoid interference. This strategy helps local staff gain credibility within the organization and confidence that they can successfully execute a strategy.

The second element of a regional office's role is to act as a commercial intelligence system. A commercial intelligence system is the key to implementing a successful business strategy. Firms lacking an intelligence system operate in the dark and make decisions that are not based on facts.

To build a commercial intelligence system, a company must study the marketplace thoroughly and develop a system for gathering and analyzing information. Manufacturing companies are accustomed to this process, but the investment management business often neglects this important function. Many investment management companies make decisions based on assumptions rather than research and study of the marketplace. Developing a good intelligence system outside the United States is particularly difficult without a high-quality local staff.

Southeast Asian Client Environment

The Southeast Asian client environment has two important features. First, because the Southeast Asian capital markets are still developing, investors there are different from most U.S. investors. Bangkok, Singapore, and Kuala Lumpur are developed, urbanized areas with sophisticated clients. Most Southeast Asian investors, however, are not familiar with modern portfolio theory, nor are they interested in it.

By and large, most of the large investors in Southeast Asia are Chinese businessmen who have developed their wealth through a combination of industrial enterprise—ownership of a local company—and accumulation of real estate. Real estate is probably the most important element in building capital throughout Southeast Asia. Virtually every wealthy family or group has substantial real estate assets. These investors have a completely different approach than U.S. investors to the way they invest. Their ownership of a company and associated real estate is their main asset; ownership of shares is a sideline endeavor.

Investors in this region have a gambling approach to the stock market that is often not based on fundamentals. The Southeast Asian markets are extremely volatile; the Hong Kong market has the highest standard deviation of any market in the world. Local investors know

the markets are volatile, and their investment approach is driven by local knowledge, trend following, and speculative fever. Westerners cannot assume that the rational approach applies; in fact, it usually does not. For example, in Hong Kong at the end of the horse racing season, virtually every second-line and speculative stock increases in value because billions of dollars leave the racetrack and go into the stock market.

The distinction between corporate and personal wealth is blurred in Southeast Asia. The largest companies are dominated by family groups. Their assets and the assets of the company are intermingled. The owners of those assets, whether they are representing the corporation or themselves, behave like wealthy individuals. This means that even when they are representing their corporation, they do not act like U.S. pension fund sponsors.

Because of investors' gambling mentality and the realization that the markets are volatile, investment horizons are short in Southeast Asia. Investors want absolute returns rather than relative returns. Imposing a Western measurement standard, such as an index, for performance measurement is usually not appropriate because the clients are not interested in beating an index; they are interested in making themselves wealthier. This attitude has a real impact on how a portfolio management staff manages clients' assets. Often the best approach is to have a compensation system tied to a mix of absolute and relative returns.

Successful Southeast Asian Operations

As in other parts of the world, personal relationships are extremely important in Southeast Asia. Rapid staff turnover, abrupt changes in business strategy, and a loss of client confidence are usually fatal to an investment manager. Offices must have continuity of staff and strategy. A network of relationships is probably the regional office's single most valuable asset.

Establishing personal relationships in Southeast Asia can be a delicate process.

The most successful summit meetings—like those between the United States and the Soviet Union—are preceded by dozens of advance meetings to agree on the agenda, to resolve problems, and to make the kind of personal connections that will ensure the success of the final summit meeting.

The routine is no different in Southeast Asia. Investment management companies have a series of meetings between their local staff and the prospective family groups to build a relationship. Senior staff from outside the region play a ceremonial and ambassadorial role. They arrive on the scene only when the stage has been set by the local office. If the companies try to conduct business without advance prepara-

tion, success is unlikely. The leader of a large corporation or large family group has to develop consensus within his family and company before deciding to give an investment firm assets to manage.

Conclusion

Creating a successful international effort requires three key actions: build a long-term, consistent business strategy; stick to it; and use local staff both to modify the strategy and to execute it. Also, hire the best local employees possible, and train them. They must have power within the organization, and the organization must learn from them rather than dictating to them.

Accounting, Traditions, and Culture

Hugh Aldous
Managing Partner
Robson Rhodes

Because international accounting differences are not merely about the nuts and bolts of who adopts which depreciation system, financial analysts must acquire a mental filter through which to look when comparing sets of accounts. One such filter is an understanding of the attitudes and values that underpin the accounting system.

Accounting is as much a reflection of national culture as it is of anything else. A brief reflection on the past 150 years or so will illustrate this point.

The English originally made their money as buccaneers and industrialists. They developed a way of life so aggressive that, even today, more people in the United States trace their origins to England than to any other country. The British (English, Scots, Irish, and Welsh) colonized countries all over the world, obliging them to purchase their goods from England.

Wherever the English colonized, their accountants went, too. Some accountants stayed predominantly in England—namely, Mr. Peat, Mr. Deloitte, Mr. Price, and Mr. Waterhouse—and dispatched colleagues to faraway places. Others were part of the great exodus themselves. In the United States, some bright Scots and English accountants set up shop. Their names pepper the U.S. profession—Mr. Young, Mr. Touche, Mr. Marwick, and Mr. Mitchell, among others.

Meanwhile, in many more law-abiding countries—mainly in Europe—life continued in a more orderly manner. The English were kept at bay, and their accountants were politely shown the door or were obliged to speak a foreign language, which had the same effect. Separate worlds developed: those of the Anglo-American culture and those of more disciplined and controlled environments.

The English are great brokers and traders. The Scots are too, to an extent, but on the whole, they would rather be the bankers. The English developed elaborate means to finance merchants and adventurers, and they developed an active free economy, which led the world with the first industrial revolution. Others who came later probably did things better, but the immense prosperity of Great Britain in the 19th century was phenomenal, even by current U.S. standards.

The sheer wealth of Britain 150 years ago was astonishing. As a proportion of the world's wealth, it has never been equalled. Naturally, the English needed accountants, and their influence was considerable. In the 1840s and 1850s, the rate of wealth creation and industrial adventure led to the development of those great inventions, the joint stock company and the public shareholder. Only as the economy began to decline and people began to argue over the remains were lawyers needed.

The French had an excellent general named Napoleon. He caused the English several difficulties, which resulted in income taxation in Britain and a clear codification of law in France, both leading to the codification of accounts. Other countries developed similar ideas. The Prussians (a slightly dour form of German) codified their version of Roman law, which led to their version of codified accounts. The Japanese then took a liking to the Prussian way of codifying law. The English did what they liked, while everyone else started to be more formal and do as they were told. The Scots and the Dutch, of course, continued to be bankers through the whole operation, risking very little themselves but making vast profits in the middle.

So 150 years ago, the British were making it up as they went along, the French and the Germans were beginning to specify what it was people had to do before they did it, and the Japanese were getting their first taste of having a look at what someone else does—and doing it better.

The Impact of Accounting Traditions

Accounting began to give different forms and context to business. The culture, language, and assumptions in the eyes and minds of readers of Swedish, German, or Japanese accounts are quite different from those of readers of a set of U.K. or U.S. accounts. International accounting differences are not merely about the nuts and bolts of who adopts which inventory valuation method or depreciation system. The differences have a history and a current business environment around them. Differences exist in the minds of the people who strive to recognize profit in the accounting statements they prepare, and they are also in the eyes of the reader. A good analyst has to acquire that variable mental filter through which he looks at comparable sets of accounts. One variable mental filter is an understanding of the attitudes and values that underpin the accounting system.

■ *Attitude toward value.* Fifty years ago, when economists were respectable and had passable reputations, one of their leaders, Keynes, said he would far rather be approximately right than be an accountant and be precisely wrong. This witticism underlies an attitude toward value: Should accountants try to be approximately right according to today's values, or should they record precisely what was known to be right at one time and not meddle with it thereaf-

ter? For example, once a fixed asset is in the books in Germany or the United States, that is it, and the accounting policies follow. In the United Kingdom, it can be meddled with.

■ *Attitude toward authority.* In Germany, France, and other countries that have codified their laws and, to a great extent, their accounts, the idea is largely that the same set of accounts serves the purposes of the tax authorities and of correct reporting for purposes of stewardship. Matters are strictly laid out, and accountancy is more a science than an art. The Italians, who are naturally artistic, keep two sets of accounts: one for themselves, and one for the tax man.

■ *Attitude toward creditors.* In the Anglo-Saxon world, the large number of limited companies and the hands-off attitude of banks lead to a large number of failures at times of economic downturn. Therefore, political expediency requires making a good deal of noise about creditor protection. Creditor protection has been a theme of the Anglo-American world, which has been an adventurous one, by and large, raising large amounts of capital by issuing shares or, as you call it, stock.

■ *Attitude toward audit.* The first sign of deterioration in an economy is probably when people do not want to make anything but would rather be accountants, lawyers, or research analysts. Nevertheless, the excesses of the Anglo-American way of doing business led to the advisability of auditors and, in turn, a profession that rapidly got the idea that it had better stay a step ahead of the game to avoid government intervention.

Government Regulation

In the United States, the market situation became uncomfortable earlier than in the United Kingdom, and thus the Securities and Exchange Commission (SEC) was formed in 1934. The British got away without serious interference until the late 1960s, when a number of scandals caused them to put their house in order. We are still trying to do that. Although the profession has "lost the ball," the government has studiously avoided picking it up, so a body similar to the Financial Accounting Standards Board (FASB) was created to kick things along a bit farther.

The outcome, greatly simplified, is that many of the countries of continental Europe have uniform charts of accounts, whereas the Anglo-Americans are more flexible, disinclined to use charts or coded accounts and more prone to provide extensive information in notes. The British, so far, are a little less inclined to prescribe every detail. Neither tradition went out of the way to compile a set of accounts with the user in mind.

The Anglo-Americans seek a concept of "present fairly" and frown upon excessive, arbitrary reserves. The continental Europeans tend to be more conservative, requiring legal reserves and encouraging tax-based reserves (although, curiously, some allow the revaluation of fixed assets, which the United States and Japan do not). The British and their commonwealth followers allow the revaluation of fixed assets on a rather casual basis.

Who calls the shots in this process? In France, Germany, and Japan, it is the government through the law. In the United Kingdom and the British commonwealth, the law has some influence, but the main influence comes from the accountancy bodies. In the United States, a most interesting interplay has developed between the SEC and the independent FASB; between them, they call the shots.

Viewpoints Toward Accounting

Generally, Japanese, French, and German accounts tend to be conservative, both in their statements of asset values and in their statements of earnings. Accounts in the United States tend to be judgmental but within the context of an enormous number of bulletins, opinions, standards, and releases. Accounts in the United Kingdom are also judgmental and are biased toward optimism; they have come to be viewed with a little cynicism.

Some of the differences in the range between conservative and optimistic accounts is reflected in the different price–earnings ratios of shares in the different markets. An old U.K. accounting joke poses the question, "What's the profit?" The reply is, "What figure did you have in mind?" To some extent, this principle is still operative.

About 10 years ago, I was taken to task by a merchant bank with a client that had achieved some results that surprised the market. The merchant bank's director said, "I thought it was the job of the auditor to try to help his client take a view of one year with another and not present the market with surprises like this." This is an interesting concept of auditing: anticipating and avoiding surprises.

Anglo-American accounting, by and large, may serve more-mature markets well. The thinking is derived from English law—adapt the system as you go along. It tries to reflect substance over form and concerns itself with the shareholder. It tries to answer the question, "How are we doing?" It does not in itself serve the interests of government. If an accountant has to adjust the accounts to a set of government rules to draw up tax computations, so be it.

The Continental view tends more toward "correct" results according to a set of rules and codes. The result is not intended, particularly, to tell the shareholder how the business is doing or to help anybody decide what dividend to declare. It is intended to complete a process correctly.

Above these legalistic and formative influences are some strong institutional attitudes. For example, in several countries, the state actively encourages various forms of investment reserves, tax-free reserves, or other means for business to retain funds. Other countries parade something of a travesty of this with forms of "fiscal investments." Nevertheless, the intention is to encourage savings.

The difference in attitude between the German or Japanese banks and U.K. or U.S. banks is well known. Curiously, the short-term, arms-length attitude of U.K. banks does not lead to more conservative accounting. It leads to the opposite: window dressing or virtually false accounts prefaced by the remark, "If we were more conservative, we would alarm our bankers or breach our covenants."

The consequence of many of the issues addressed thus far starts to show in an attitude toward accounts and accounting. In some countries, the attitude fosters long-term retention of value within corporations. In others, businesses are actively encouraged to generate maximum short-term earnings per share, take a short-term attitude, and dress up the balance sheet. I believe that some of the arguments about what is extraordinary (annoyingly, the word in French is *exceptionnel*), what is continuing or discontinued, and what is earned in each segment of the business involves the British obsession with showing short-term results in the best possible light.

What is Profit?

From a nonanalyst point of view, profit may be recognized in at least three different ways. A lawyer may recognize profit if a distributable surplus exists. Both an accountant and an economist may believe that if two balance sheets are restated on fairly consistent principles—one balance sheet at each end of the relevant period of time—then profit would be the difference between the two. The problem is that the economist would restate everything, but the accountant would only put through those adjustments that can be faithfully reflected in the company's ledgers. Other economists, and increasingly some accountants, may recognize profit if a business demonstrates surplus cash flow or an increase in net present value of future cash flows.

Finally, a grand tug-of-war exists between accountants and auditors over extraordinary items.

Differences in Accounting Practices

Some issues affecting "profit" are revenue recognition and some of the more basic nuts and bolts of sets of accounts.
■ *Revenue recognition.* Revenue can be recognized in at least a half-dozen ways. For example, in cases of royalty income, or when applying the percentage-of-completion method to construction contracts, revenue is recognized during production. When applying the completed-contract method, referring to such processes as growing agricultural produce, revenue is not normally recognized until the completion of production. In most sales contracts, revenue is recognized at the time of sale, but for some goods and most services, that does not happen until delivery.

For goods shipped subject to certain conditions, revenue may not be recognized until after delivery, and if an after-sales service is provided—some sort of franchise arrangement or fee basis—revenue may not be recognized until spread on an apportionment. In some housebuilding developments (and some currency positions), revenue is recognized on received income regardless of what is happening to the capital value of the fundamental assets or deposits. In a rather famous U.K. case, *Atlantic Computer Leasing*, revenue was recognized on a series of contracts over time regardless of the fact that the suppliers had entered into an arrangement to allow lessees to return the goods subject to certain conditions. Before tackling some of the more esoteric nuts and bolts, consider what income means.
■ *Depreciation.* One of the most commonplace items of cost should always get a second glance—depreciation. In the 1970s, British Gas (then a nationalized industry) shifted from being a relatively cheap energy provider funded by the government to being a source of very considerable cash inflow to the Treasury—while reporting consistently modest profits so as not to distress the public.

The changes in the British Gas depreciation policy were fairly dramatic, and to a prepared and informed audience, simply reading out the accounting policies year by year, plus the auditors' perfectly clean audit report, could reduce grown men to tears of mirth. The government, having soaked the public for as much as it could one way, then soaked it again by selling it back its own asset—almost as soon as the extent of its profitability became evident.

Although depreciation has a large impact on the other accounts, it is probably the most inconsistently applied standard in the world. In both the United Kingdom and the United States, most companies choose to account for depreciation on the straight-line method, and the notes to the accounts are supposed to provide enough information to work out whether the straight-line periods are as expected. Japan allows accelerated depreciation, as does Germany. Germany and most north European countries allow excess depreciation.

■ *Inventory valuation.* Every accountant putting together a compilation of accounts of a small business for tax purposes knows that one item with a massive effect on profits is the inventory valuation.

In the United Kingdom, inventory will be valued on the first-in, first-out (FIFO) basis because of the Statement of Standard Accounting Practice 9 and because doing it any other way is pointless (the Inland Revenue will not accept last-in, first-out [LIFO], the old favorite in the United States). Note that U.S. accounts, in some cases, have become so distorted by the use of LIFO that the SEC now requires companies to disclose the replacement cost of inventory and the effect on profits of any inventory reduction. In the U.S. accounts of larger corporations, the notes will probably reveal the effect of using LIFO for inventory. In France, LIFO is not permitted. Germany permits LIFO, and a general theme of being conservative and abiding by tax rules underlies inventory valuation. Curiously, administrative overheads may be included in inventory values in Germany, but not in the United Kingdom.

Inventory valuations in the United Kingdom are at the lower of cost and net realizable value. In Germany, they are the lowest of historical cost, net realizable value, current replacement cost, or other lower value. In Switzerland, they are total cost less 25 percent.

■ *Long-term contracts.* Long-term contracts are valued in the United Kingdom on the percentage-of-completion basis and may include an element of profit. In France, long-term construction contracts are usually accounted for by the completion method, which recognizes profit largely when the job is complete. In Germany, long-term contract work in progress on construction and shipbuilding is valued at cost, and profit is taken only upon completion. Some companies in France and The Netherlands use the percentage-of-completion and the completed-contract methods simultaneously.

■ *Fixed assets.* France, Germany, and the United Kingdom allow revaluation of fixed assets, whereas the United States and Japan do not. In Germany, intangibles were once held at zero. Deutsche Bank's 28 percent holding in Daimler-Benz is held at 1948 cost, which is virtually zero, with no information about current value. In the United Kingdom, finance leases are capitalized—as they are, by and large, in the United States. In France, finance leases may be capitalized, but in Germany, they may not.

■ *Pension provisions.* A study of European accounts showed that only half the companies reviewed disclosed pension provisions. Of the half making disclosures, two-thirds recognized a liability and one-third simply noted their pension provisions. South American, Spanish, and some other accounts often record pension costs as the cash flows out and recognize no actuarial liability.

■ *Currency exchange.* The Germans are the main exponents of the temporal method of currency translation, in which assets are translated into the currency for which accounts are consolidated. The exchange rate used is the rate prevailing when the assets were purchased, irrespective of the consolidation date. Other countries have moved either to average rates for the profit and loss account and closing or to current rates for the balance sheet or current rates generally.

This method, of course, produces a nonsense result for assets such as land acquired in countries where the currency has been devalued since the purchase. In the United Kingdom, accountants may revalue fixed assets in the balance sheet, so that particular nonsense pertains particularly to U.K. balance sheets. I detect a growing movement in the United States seeking to allow assets to be revalued—better, after all, to be more nearly right than precisely wrong.

■ *Reserves.* Reserve accounting has been deplored for some time. In the United Kingdom, goodwill on acquisition is written off against reserves, but the earnings from the business acquired will subsequently pass through the profit and loss account without any matching amortization. This practice has gone on long enough. Too many U.K. companies that have generated some general reserves by one means or another write off much of the cost of acquisitions without that cost being particularly obvious and then take all subsequent earnings as part of earnings per share.

In the United Kingdom, expense provisions are usually for past events with future costs. German and French accounts have provisions for risks and contingencies so they can smooth profits between years. In the mid-1980s, AEG reported profits of exactly zero for three years running. That use of provisions is illegal in the United Kingdom. Belgium, France, Germany, Italy, and Spain require statutory and legal reserves.

■ *Consolidated accounts.* In Germany, consolidation is not yet widespread, and not all subsidiaries are consolidated. Also in Germany, control of a company may not be by majority shareholding but by contract, a legal arrangement whereby one party, irrespective of shareholding, is given absolute control.

France usually values contracts under the completed-contract method, but in consolidated accounts, they can use the U.K. method—percentage of completion. The consolidated accounts are not used for tax purposes, and they are the ones that are used internationally.

■ *Bad debts.* Accounting for bad debts is a highly variable "tide" of events. That is a great game among the U.K. banks, which must be either telepathic or equally as bad as each other or else they ring each other up and decide among them to have a common line on their level of bad debts. In some recent notorious cases, bank debts have proven to be totally fictitious anyway.

■ *Securities.* The way securities are shown is another area of difference. Market value is allowed in the United Kingdom and certain other countries.

■ *Other intangibles.* Accounting for intangibles varies by country. In the United Kingdom, goodwill is usually written off against reserves on the basis of "now you see it, now you don't"; in the United States, it must be capitalized and written off over a useful life of up to 40 years. A trend has begun in the United Kingdom to value brands in the balance sheet—but whether they are worth anything and how quickly the value of the name could collapse are uncertain.

Development expenditure is normally written off but in some cases can be carried forward as an asset to be written off against specific future sales if a project can be gauged at the outset as having a high probability of commercial success. The requirements for assessing commercial success can vary widely within a country and between countries.

Software costs can be capitalized in France and Germany, but generally they are not in the United Kingdom or the United States.

■ *Off-balance-sheet financing.* In many cases, off-balance-sheet financing conceals controlled associated companies or finance subsidiaries that are not consolidated. Despite European Community directives and the 1989 Companies Act, those arrangements are becoming more common in the United Kingdom. In the United States, General Motors only recently began to consolidate its finance subsidiary. At the current rate of progress by General Motors, its manufacturing arm may become a fairly irrelevant part of its finance operations.

■ *Taxes.* Taxes have always been a fascinating conundrum. In the United Kingdom, taxes will be provided for only to the extent that it is foreseeable they will have to be paid. Deferred taxes are provided in the United Kingdom, the United States, and to some extent in France, whereas deferred tax provisions generally do not occur in Germany or Japan. All these observations proceed on the assumption that an international group has already made up its mind on the grand scheme of things such as where it wants its profits to arise and whether the tax authorities could find that out.

Future Accounting Standards

The Holy Grail, internationally harmonized accounting standards, is worth striving for. Constant analytical commentary by investment managers will help that process. All of the major countries are showing some tendency for change.

The United States seems to be becoming more prescriptive in the way values are expressed through accounts, while the United Kingdom is becoming less prescriptive in detail and more strongly conceptual. It has a new body called the Accounting Standards Board, which is at last a free-standing organization and not a club meeting of the "Big 6" technical partners. It might achieve what the FASB and the SEC have jointly achieved in the United States but with one-tenth the number of pronouncements.

My French partners would never admit for one moment that they have the slightest interest in going the way of the United Kingdom. If they have any sympathies in one direction or another, it is to become less prescriptive and conceivably slightly Anglo-American. Germany and Japan seem to be content in the happy knowledge that they are right and we are wrong. U.S. Generally Accepted Accounting Principles (GAAP) have been exerting a tremendous international pull, and restatement to U.S. GAAP seems increasingly commonplace.

I hope the standards being developed by the International Accounting Standards Committee (IASC) will have great influence. Meanwhile, all sorts of hybrid additional statements abound in published accounts. Some accountants provide a complete supplementary financial statement in GAAP or reconcile their present accounting statements to GAAP; others do little more than translate some words into U.S. English, give figures in dollars, or confuse everyone with a limited restatement of their accounts.

Conclusion

Accounting is important, as evidenced by the way users are trying to redress the current state of confusion. A recent study showed that translating the stated distributable profits of Spanish Telephones under various different accounting principles produced wildly different figures. The Center for International Financial Analysis and Research each year compares various large companies under different accounting principles. This study certainly highlights the lower operating margin of Japanese companies reporting under Japanese accounting standards compared to U.S. accounting standards. How far that difference explains the higher price–earnings ratios in the Japanese market is difficult to judge.

Of course, one solution is to disentangle the whole lot of differing national accounts back to simple cash flow statements, report results in direct cash flows, and evaluate companies as a multiple of cash flow.

The Scots have been persuasive recently in trying to take a fresh look at accounts. The Scottish Institute concluded:

- All financial reports should reflect economic reality.
- The information investors need is the same in kind, but not in volume, as the information managements need to run their entities.
- Some information that management possesses, but does not normally communicate, comes out into the open when management wants something—such as additional capital or to defend against a hostile takeover bid.
- Financial reports are deficient in that they are based on legal form rather than economic substance, on cost rather than value, on the past rather than the future, and on profit rather than wealth.
- The production of profit and loss accounts and balance sheets has no consistent conceptual basis.

■ The audit report is insufficiently informative and often incomprehensible to nonauditors.

The world of accounting standards needs to be taken in hand. The United States has recognized 53 exposure drafts from one or another eminent body. No one can possibly cope with that. U.S. accounting standards are starting to slide into a massive volume of directions.

The IASC has managed to reduce its work load to manageable proportions by producing a relatively small number of standards that began as optional approaches. It is becoming more prescriptive and quite well balanced in its approach, and I hope it will become a widely recognized, globally influential body. Meanwhile, international accounting standards are becoming widely accepted in several of the emerging markets.

Accounting standards are an area in which organizations like the Association for Investment Management and Research can bring some pressure to bear internationally. Accounts should be understandable by the reasonably educated reader and capable of being compared among countries. Global investors and analysts need comparable information. Inefficient information leads to inefficient decisions and inefficient allocation of resources. We should try to encourage this important economic area to become more enlightened.

Geographical Perspectives on Investment Opportunities in Europe

Alexander B. Murphy
Associate Professor of Geography
University of Oregon

Culture and investment involve much more than the matters normally associated with a cultural awareness workshop. In fact, culture is at the heart of the investment process, and geography provides significant insight into just how.

The idea of looking at culture and investment together was not a popular one a few years ago. Our thinking was dominated by economic models that largely held cultural differences constant. Events in the past few years, however, have challenged conventional assumptions.

Culture is an important variable in international investment and is revealed at many levels. At the simplest level, we usually think of awareness of local customs. The conventional wisdom is that you do not go to Damascus and invite your hosts out for a dinner of roast suckling pig, and you do not send a battery of lawyers to initiate a business contact in Japan. These are important things to know, but culture and investment involve much more than the matters normally associated with a cultural awareness workshop. In fact, culture is at the heart of the investment process, and geography provides significant insight into just how.

Importance of Geography

Most of us accept the notion that history is fundamentally shaped by culture. Sometimes, however, we fail to recognize that history is not just events and personalities but conscious and unconscious decisions about where people live, which resources are exploited, and where industries are located. In other words, part of cultural history is the creation of a human geography—the array of patterns, regions, and places that characterize the world at any given moment.

The study of international economics has largely ignored the significance of human geography for economic processes. The resulting myopia of much international economic theory now is being exposed. Paul Krugman, in his recent book on geography and trade, directly challenges the ageographical character of international economic theory.[1] He argues that economic form cannot be understood without considering the decisive role of history in determining the geography of real economies. He attributes considerable causal significance to this geography in explaining economic change.

European Geography

Maps of language and religions, population distribution, concentrations of industry, and human-induced environmental change show cultural geographic factors that are fundamentally shaping economic developments and trends in Europe.

Languages

A linguistic perspective of Europe is presented in **Figure 1**. Even in simpli-

[1]Paul Krugman, *Geography and Trade* (Leuven: Leuven University Press, and Cambridge: The MIT Press, 1991).

31

Figure 1. Languages of Europe

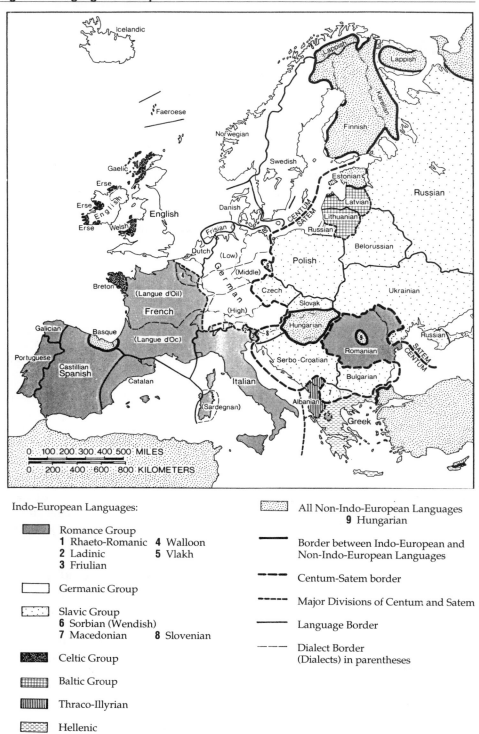

Indo-European Languages:

▨ Romance Group
  1 Rhaeto-Romanic **4** Walloon
  2 Ladinic   **5** Vlakh
  3 Friulian

☐ Germanic Group

▦ Slavic Group
  6 Sorbian (Wendish)
  7 Macedonian   **8** Slovenian

▨ Celtic Group

▦ Baltic Group

▨ Thraco-Illyrian

▨ Hellenic

▨ All Non-Indo-European Languages
  9 Hungarian

━━━ Border between Indo-European and
     Non-Indo-European Languages

━ ━ ━ Centum-Satem border

━ ━ ━ Major Divisions of Centum and Satem

━━━ Language Border

━ ━ ━ Dialect Border
     (Dialects) in parentheses

Source: Terry G. Jordan, *The European Culture Area: A Systematic Geography* 2d ed. (New York: Harper & Row, 1987), p. 94. Reprinted by permission.

fied terms, a language map is complex and does not necessarily correspond to political boundaries. In some parts of Europe, this map defines patterns of interaction and communication that can be of some importance. Language boundaries can be zones of tension, as is the case in Belgium, where French and Dutch come together. Instabilities connected with the presence of more than one language group in the same state can affect the investment environment in countries as diverse as Spain, Yugoslavia, and Czechoslovakia.

Religions

Beyond language, other overt cultural factors shape European society. One of the most obvious is religion, illustrated in **Figure 2**. This generalized map recognizes the predominance of Western Christianity throughout much of Western Europe. What we have conventionally called Eastern Europe is divided among Western Christianity, Eastern Christianity, and Islam. A map of religion is not just something of abstract interest; it provides insights into important social, and therefore economic, circumstances. Because religion reflects fundamental cultural values and historical experiences, boundaries between religious groups can be volatile. This certainly has been the case in Northern Ireland and especially in Yugoslavia, which is fragmented among Western Christians, Eastern Christians, and Moslems. Not surprisingly, when Yugoslavia descended into chaos in 1991, Western investment dried up. Yet the new state of Slovenia may well recover rapidly, building on its cultural continuities with the West. The prospects elsewhere in the former state of Yugoslavia are much more clouded.

Ethnic Zones

Language and religion are often the basis for patterns of ethnic identity. Our habit of thinking about Europe in terms of its constituent states often blinds us to the importance of ethnic zones, such as those shown in **Figure 3** for Eastern Europe. The significance of these zones for investment, however, is becoming increasingly clear. The uncertainties sur-

rounding the uneasy marriage between the Czechs and the Slovaks, for example, are discouraging Western investment in the Slovak part of Czechoslovakia. Ethnic patterns are important in Western Europe as well. Groups such as the Flemings and Walloons in Belgium and the Basques and Catalans in Spain have sought and won increasing autonomy. They are even trying to establish direct lines of communication with the European Community. Such developments are rapidly changing the economic picture in Western Europe and deserve more attention than they are generally accorded.

Political Divisions

The partitioning of Europe along Cold War lines, between East and West, was not just important politically and economically; it had a great cultural impact as well. The implications of 45 years of living under different political/economic systems can be seen in Germany with the different attitudes in East and West toward the unification process. The old Cold War boundary also had a tremendous impact on attitudes toward work, economic expectations, and personal material priorities. The geography of cultural perspectives, as much or more than crude economic indicators, will shape the economic restructuring of Europe in the 1990s.

Population

Among the other elements of European geography that are cultural creations is the basic pattern of population itself (**Figure 4**). This pattern reflects a variety of factors that historically have affected where people live. One is where food could be grown, although different cultures have different views of what kinds of food should be grown and what environment is suitable for it. Population distribution maps reflect patterns of cultural history—the places people have viewed as appropriate to settle. These places in turn reveal much about patterns of economic activity and the location of markets.

Economics

By looking at the population map to-

Figure 2. Major Religions of Europe

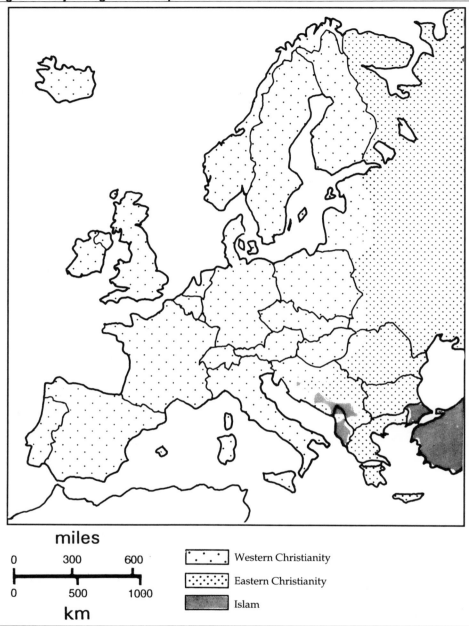

miles

0	300	600
0	500	1000

km

[. . .] Western Christianity

[::::::] Eastern Christianity

[▓▓] Islam

Source: Alexander B. Murphy and Gil Latz, "Geography and International Studies," *Revealing the World: An Interdisciplinary Reader for International Studies*, D. Lieberman and M. Gurtov, eds. Copyright 1992 by Kendall/Hunt Publishing Co. Reprinted with permission.

gether with an economic map of Europe (**Figure 5**), certain patterns emerge— core areas with high population concentration and heavy industrial activity, and peripheral areas with the obverse configuration. Different types of economic forces are at play in core and peripheral areas; the former are areas of considerable economic momentum, whereas the latter risk being left behind in the move toward a more integrated European economy.

Figure 3. Ethnic Boundaries in Former Eastern Europe

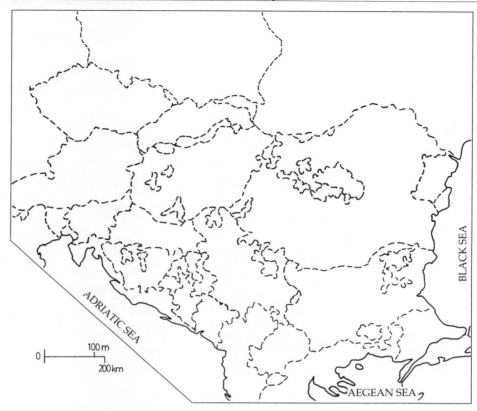

Source: Alexander B. Murphy.

Significance of Cultural Geography

The nature and significance of the patterns revealed in Figures 1 through 5 are often overlooked because of the tendency to think solely about the prospects of individual states. Profiles of individual states are important, of course, but basic geographic patterns of language, religion, ethnicity, demography, and economy frequently do not follow state boundaries. They operate along with state-based patterns to shape the economic and investment environments in Europe.

The patterns considered thus far are very general, of course, but much can be learned from looking at the patterns revealed on maps of this sort. Take, for example, the map of religion in Europe. When thinking about the establishment of links between Eastern and Western Europe, the cultural fault line dividing Western Christianity from Eastern

Christianity and Islam may not seem important, but we have seen the importance of this line in Yugoslavia during the past year. On a large scale, the line separates areas with fundamentally Western historical influences from those subject to Eastern Orthodox and Ottoman Turkish historical/cultural influences. This significant difference can be seen in the divergent paths countries have taken toward democratization and privatization. Western political and economic norms have been much quicker to develop in Poland, Czechoslovakia, Hungary, Slovenia, and Croatia than in other parts of Eastern Europe.

What the Yugoslav example suggests is that a consideration of basic geographic patterns and, more generally, a perspective that looks beyond the fortunes of individual states is important if we are to understand better the cultural context of investment in Europe. To

Figure 4. Population Density in Europe

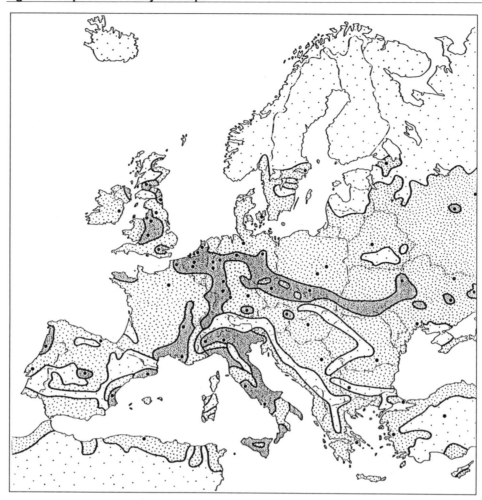

Population Density

Per Square Mile		Per Square Kilometer
Over 250		Over 100
60 – 250		25 – 100
Under 60		Under 25

• Cities with over one million inhabitants

Source: Terry G. Jordan, *The European Culture Area: A Systematic Geography* 2d ed. (New York:. Harper & Row, 1987), p. 150. Reprinted by permission.

illustrate the point, examine three key contemporary developments in Europe: regional economic shifts following the fall of the Iron Curtain, the spillover effects of European integration, and the emergence of the environment as a significant social and economic issue.

Investments in Post-Cold-War Europe

On a small scale, we can see the importance of cultural differences within various countries for patterns of investment. Patterns of Western investment are very

Figure 5. Economic Geography of Europe

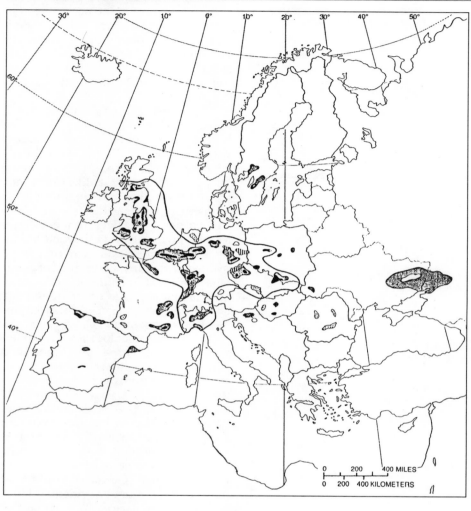

Manufacturing Centers

Industrial Region

Bituminous Coalfield

Lignite Field

Petroleum and Natural Gas

Limits of Europe's
Industrial Heartland

Source: James R. McDonald, *The European Scene: A Geographic Perspective* (Englewood Cliffs: Prentice Hall, 1992), p. 190.

hard to reconstruct because most data are reported only at the state level. Moreover, more refined data are incomplete and spotty. Nevertheless, reports in *Business Eastern Europe* make possible the construction of investment maps such as that shown for Czechoslovakia in **Figure 6**. The map covers a nine-month period during 1990 and 1991. In a crude way, Figure 6 provides a sense of the concentration of investment in capital cities and, to some extent, in western Czechoslovakia.

The patterns of Western investment in Czechoslovakia reflect a bias toward the western part of the country. The concentration of investment in western Czechoslovakia is reminiscent of other cultural geographic patterns in Czechoslovakia, one of them being literacy (see

Figure 6. Western Investment and Trade Agreements with Czechoslovak Firms, August 1990–May 1991

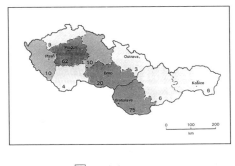

☐ 1 – 9 Agreements

▨ 10 – 19 Agreements

■ 20+ Agreements

Source: Based on reports in *Business Eastern Europe.*

Figure 7, showing library loan rates), a surrogate for levels of education. With the concentration of investment in western Czechoslovakia, that part of the country may prosper much more than areas farther east. This has obvious implications for state stability, because the Slovaks in the east are likely to feel as if they are being left behind.

More generally, the Iron Curtain was not just a border separating countries; it was also a zone of stagnation. Regions along the old West–East divide were on the margins of the two major political/economic systems that dominated

Figure 7. Annual Library Loans per Person, Czechoslovakia

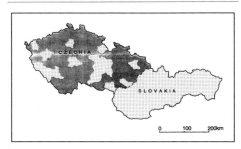

▨ Less than Three per Person

■ Greater than or Equal to Three per Person

Source: Atlas Ceskoslovenské Socialistické Republiky, 1966, p. 57.

Europe, but they were peripheral to both. Thus, most of the poorest regions in former West Germany—those eligible for European Community economic development assistance—were concentrated along the divide between West Germany and East Germany/Czechoslovakia.

The German example suggests that as the former divide between West and East loses its significance, border areas will be ripe for growth. This is already beginning to happen. Plans are being made in West and East alike to upgrade the transportation and communication infrastructure along the former West–East border. The effects of renewed interaction will extend far beyond border regions; tremendous growth has already occurred in the shipment of goods out of the port of Hamburg, which can now take advantage of traffic moving down the Elbe River corridor from former East Germany and Czechoslovakia.

Applying similar locational considerations on a larger scale, Germany is clearly in a particularly strategic position to benefit from developing links between West and East. Most trade between Poland, Czechoslovakia, and Hungary, on the one hand, and Western Europe, on the other, will pass through Germany. Germany is also in an excellent position to access markets to the East. As such, Germany could well move to the center of a widening European economic space. To assume that this will happen overnight, however, is to ignore the enormous problems Germany faces in the unification process— problems that are likely to plague the German economy for the next decade. Moreover, economic recovery in Eastern Europe is likely to be slow at best, in no small part because of the cultural legacy of a half-century of Soviet domination.

Economic Integration Within the European Community

The movement toward economic integration within the West has precipitated a rapid rise in interstate trade. Just as important as the general features of a centralized European economy are the spillover effects of integration. In one sense, economic integration promotes economies of scale, whether in industry, such as in the Ruhr Valley, or in agriculture, such as in the large-scale agriculture of the north European plain. These economies of scale are most likely to develop in places that for cultural/historical reasons have a head start. The danger is that in the long run, having the rich get richer and the poor get poorer could be destabilizing for Western Europe.

Transportation costs, though not great, will help to protect the periphery of the European Community to some degree, and specialized industries that have a head start in the periphery may thrive. Southern Italy, northern Greece, northern Portugal, and northeastern Spain, however, may well have severe economic difficulties in the years ahead unless the European Community channels significant regional development funds to these areas.

A particularly interesting spillover effect of the integration process that is often neglected is the growth of economic and cultural links among regions in different countries. **Figure 8** shows some of the links that are developing among regions on either side of international boundaries. Some of the strongest of these are occurring in places where the same language is spoken on either side of the border. In many cases, the links are still tenuous, but they are growing. Moreover, the European Community has adopted new, innovative programs to encourage such links. The economic benefits of cross-border cooperation are already evident around Geneva and Basel. The development of closer links between French and German regions along the upper Rhine and between Spanish and French regions bordering the Mediterranean are likely to produce significant economic growth in those areas as well.

Environmental and Social Considerations

One of the most pressing issues in Europe today is the state of the environment. Once again, meaningful patterns do not correspond with state boundaries. The key issue is the almost 40 years of total environmental neglect in Eastern Europe, which has produced conditions so serious they cannot be ignored. Problems range from dying forests to health disasters in certain Czechoslovakian villages where background radiation levels from uranium mining during the Communist era are far above what is considered safe. Against this backdrop, it is not surprising that environmental concerns played a significant role in the democratic revolutions in Eastern Europe.

During the past two years, the difficulties of economic restructuring have focused attention away from the environment, but in the years ahead, this issue will probably reemerge as one of great importance. Hence, investment in industries seen as contributing to environmental degradation is risky, because such industries are likely to be confronted with increasingly intense local political pressure. At the same time, investment in pollution control and cleanup technology offers considerable potential. From the perspective of the social environment, one of the most important truisms of foreign investment in Europe is that investments sensitive to local culture have the best long-term prospects. This is particularly true in Eastern Europe, which is struggling to move out of the shadows of its past political domination.

Despite the enormous structural problems in Eastern Europe, this area has considerable economic potential, ranging from the agricultural productivity of the Hungarian plain to the cultural and economic vitality of capital cities such as Prague. A combination of Western status products, which have shown some potential in Eastern Europe—such as the Levi & Strauss Company's factory in Poland—and small- and medium-sized joint ventures in local products have a reasonable prospect for long-term success.

Conclusion

Knowing about the cultural context of investment is essential for assessing economic possibilities and prospects. This is true for specific decisions and for gen-

Figure 8. Cross-Border Cooperation in Western Europe

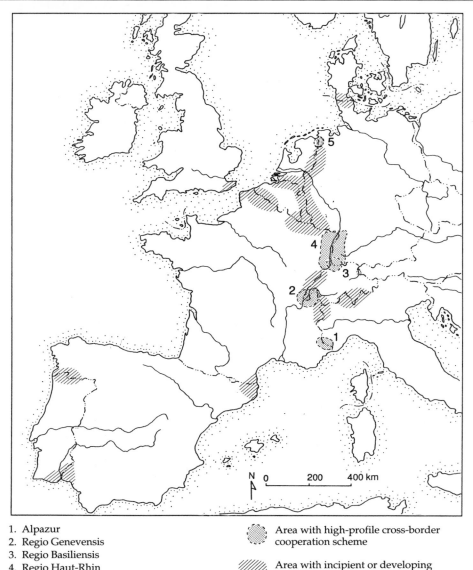

1. Alpazur
2. Regio Genevensis
3. Regio Basiliensis
4. Regio Haut-Rhin
5. Ems-Dollart Region

Area with high-profile cross-border cooperation scheme

Area with incipient or developing cross-border cooperation

Source: Alexander B. Murphy, "Emerging Regional Linkages in Europe: Implications for State-Centered Perspectives on European Society," *Tijdschrift voor Economische en Sociale Geografie.* In press.

eral strategies. As an example of the former, a business recently tried to market in Poland a product with a Russian name, because it assumed that the Poles, as Slavs, would respond to a Slavic name. This was truly an act of cultural ignorance. For centuries, the Poles have rejected almost anything having to do with Russia. At the strategy level, any attempt to evaluate an investment approach to housing in different parts of Eastern Europe is doomed to fail if it examines only the differences in the objective characteristics of houses. Such an approach would not reveal that, although housing is generally in poorer shape in Balkan Europe than farther north, the gap between expectation and reality is greater in the north. Hence, investment in northern housing is likely to have better prospects than investment in the Balkan region.

Such matters are unlikely to be recognized as significant unless we move beyond the current assumption that the state is the only region of interest. Cultural history has produced a human geography of Europe considerably more important and more subtle than conventional state-based geography would suggest. This cultural geography lies at the heart of the context from which emerge the human needs and desires that shape economic trends.

Geographical Perspectives on Investment Opportunities in the Pacific Rim

Gil Latz
Associate Professor of Geography
International Trade Institute
Portland State University

Age-old traditions and innovative thinking about the future coexist in the Pacific Rim. For analysts, the difficulty lies not in understanding the rate of change per se, but in comprehending the complex physical, cultural, and economic factors influencing attitudes toward national and regional development.

When analyzed according to diversity of cultures, economies, and climates, the Pacific Rim is the most complex region on the face of the earth. To make sense of it in the short space of this presentation and to set the foundation for addressing several of the opportunities—and the cautions to be considered—in doing business in the Pacific Rim, the objectives for this presentation must be clear from the outset.

The main points of this presentation are:

■ Economic, political, and cultural definitions of the Pacific Rim are fundamentally different.
■ The location, magnitude, and uneven distribution of population and natural resources are central to any discussion of investment opportunities in the Pacific Rim.
■ Three key problems facing Pacific Rim countries in the next 30 years are urban infrastructure development, food security, and environmental pollution.
■ The region's capacity to respond to these challenges will be uneven because of differing economic development priorities

and diverse physical geography.

Among the cultural characteristics of the Pacific Rim investment environment to be underscored:

■ Customs shape business relationships in the Asian Pacific region. Competitive pricing of a service or product is assumed; quality and long-term reliability are what will "clinch the deal."
■ Just as every country's landscape is different, so too is its attitude toward investment. Successful investors will be connoisseurs of such differences, using their understanding and appreciation of market complexity as a critical selling point in forging business relationships.
■ Japan will play an increasingly important role in the Pacific Rim as a cultural and economic epicenter, a model of infrastructure development, and a source of capital. Of the newly industrializing economies, Hong Kong, Korea, Taiwan, Singapore, and Thailand will be major competitors.

It is important to communicate from the outset some sense of the unique complexity of the Pacific region, which is now the object of so much world, and especially U.S., curiosity. One highly efficient but underappreciated (and underutilized) method for describing and analyzing this world region is by means of mapped data, which provide a common informational base for discussion of Pacific Rim trends and developments, heretofore and into the 21st century.

As the Cold War ends, and the ideology of communism is rejected by increasing numbers of people, the economic, social, and political maps of Europe change almost daily. The pace of change appears less rapid in the Pacific Rim. This observation can be deceptive, however, because one distinguishing characteristic of the non-Western world is that continuity and change are juxtaposed quite differently. Generally, the Pacific is a distinctive region where age-old traditions and innovative thinking about the future coexist. In short, the difficulty of understanding this part of the world is not the rate of change per se, but the necessity of comprehending the complex physical, cultural, and economic factors influencing attitudes toward and policies for national and regional development.

Geographical Context

The geography of the Pacific Rim is immense, as illustrated in **Figure 1**. If the Pacific Rim refers to all states and land masses contained in, bordering on, or adjacent to the Pacific Ocean, it covers approximately half the earth. The Pacific region's complexity is well illustrated by recognizing that it contains:

- the largest ocean, the Pacific, which covers approximately one-third of the earth and is roughly twice the size of the Atlantic;
- the world's tallest mountain above sea level, Mt. Everest, and largest elevated uplands, the Tibetan plateau;
- an apparently inhospitable environment for supporting a large percentage of the world's population, including extensive and rugged mountainous uplands, and in the lowlands, where population is concentrated, only moderately fertile soils and an agriculture, by and large, more dependent on water than on soil;
- huge reserves of unevenly distributed natural resources, both on land and below the sea, partic-

Figure 1. Pacific Basin—Political Geography

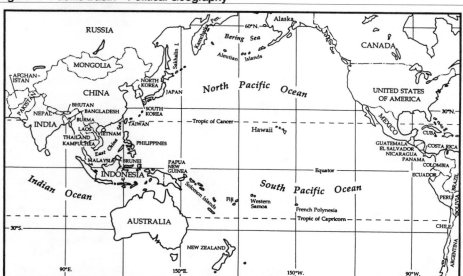

Source: Mark Borthwick and Gil Latz, *The Pacific Century Study Guide/Faculty Manual* (Boulder, Colorado: Westview Press, 1992).

ularly in the Siberian region of the former Soviet Union, the border areas of China, and in the Exclusive Economic Zones that lay claim to the seabed adjacent to the Pacific Basin and rimland countries;

- the longest-lived state in the history of the world, China;
- the largest population concentration of any country in the world, in China, approximately 1.1 billion (and, in greater Asia, the second largest population, in India), which may be contrasted to Nauru, a Pacific island state with fewer than 10,000 people and a land area of 30 square miles;
- the fastest growing cities in the world, with predictions that by the year 2000, 13 of the world's 20 largest urban agglomerations will be located in the Asian Pacific region (up from 8 of 20 in 1970);
- the only non-Western country, Japan, to attain great power status; and, of course,
- the United States, one of the most remarkable and remarked upon economic and political powers of modern history.

Indeed, the Asian Pacific region alone, what may be described as the western Pacific Rim, contains about 57 percent of the world's population, highly urbanized (nearly half of the world's urban population), stretching from Pakistan to Japan, residing in perhaps the most diverse set of cultural and physical environments on the earth's surface. It is a region, furthermore, where a number of states—Pakistan, Nepal, Afghanistan, Malaysia, Indonesia, and the Philippines—are expected to double their populations in the next 30 or 35 years.

Changing Trade Patterns

Of course, the tendency these days, especially in the United States, is to think about the Pacific in purely (and narrowly) economic terms. Pacific Rim trade has grown dramatically in importance in the past four decades. This is one of the most important international trends and developments of the latter half of the 20th century because it represents a fundamental structural change now occurring in the world economy—a shift of the world's center of economic gravity from Atlantic to Pacific. Since 1960, two-thirds of the world's economic growth has been concentrated in this region. In the early 1980s, trade between the United States and other Pacific countries surpassed that across the Atlantic. Today, an estimated 40 percent ($8 trillion) of the world's gross national product is generated by the United States and Japan ($5 trillion and $3 trillion, respectively).

This watershed change in trade between the United States and Pacific Basin countries is cause for analysis and concern—analysis because some of the most important and rapidly growing economies in the world are found in the western Pacific, representing valuable consumer markets for U.S. products, and concern because the flow of goods and services across the Pacific is remarkably out of balance in favor of the principal U.S. trading partners. Japan, for example, accounts for slightly less than half of the U.S. trade deficit (of about $100 billion in 1989). Of perhaps greater significance, Asian countries other than Japan—Taiwan, China, South Korea, Singapore—account for another 28 percent. Thus, Asian countries account for nearly three-quarters of the U.S. trade deficit.

The magnitude of Pacific Basin trade is impressive; it is well above trade across the Atlantic. The speed at which trade has grown is also noteworthy. What may be most interesting about the pattern of trade is that the North American interaction with the western Pacific represents interaction with an entire region, not a single country, as important as these individual countries might be. We now live in a world where multipolar connections overshadow bipolar ones. We must understand regional economic and other interactions in their cultural and environmental—as well as their political, economic, and strategic—complexity. We probably will not attain the degree of Pacific literacy that we need if our mental image of the Pacific Rim consists of little more than the notion that the Rim is a place where certain cities are found, neatly lined up north to south.

Problems Facing Pacific Rim Countries

At first glance, because of the large overall population, Asia and the Pacific may appear to be among the least urbanized regions of the world. In fact, however, they are highly urbanized places where nearly half of the world's 700 million city dwellers are believed to live. China alone has an urban population nearly equal to that of the entire United States—about 240 million people. Japan is also distinctive as a highly urbanized place. More than three-quarters of its population lives in urban settlements. The Tokyo metropolitan area contains some 32 million people, almost a quarter of Japan's population, in an area that accounts for less than 10 percent of the total land area.

As urban population grows, and as Asia further distinguishes itself as the region of the world with more than half of the world's largest cities, three challenges will tax human ingenuity: infrastructure development, food security, and environmental pollution.

■ *Infrastructure development.* Asian cities will require massive investments in transportation development, water supply, waste disposal, and housing. This problem's complexity ranges from Beijing, where water supply for agriculture in the North China plain will need to be diverted—or at least reallocated—for urban and industrial needs, to the need to provide more efficient transportation links in Bangkok, a city that has attained a level of congestion some observers claim now acts as a drag on new investment.

Japan may serve as a model for urban infrastructure development, given its long urban history as a country that boasted a city of a million inhabitants as early as the late 17th century. It embarked on the comprehensive development of its national and urban transportation infrastructure beginning in the early modern period between 1870 and 1910. Emerging from these investments was the farsighted bullet train transport mode, developed in conjunction with the 1964 Tokyo Olympics.

Land prices now act as a serious constraint to continuing infrastructure investment in Japan. Although the land bubble in Japan has burst, reports in the late 1980s indicated that downtown Tokyo residential prices reached the astronomical level of one-quarter million dollars per square meter. A consequence of such land price escalation is that land condemnation in the process of further infrastructure investment can account for as much as 99 percent of the cost of a given project.

■ *Food security.* As Asia's urban population grows, regional and domestic political stability will depend increasingly on growing international trade interdependence in agricultural commodities. Bangladesh and the Philippines already encounter serious imbalances between food production and the population's daily caloric intake needs. To the extent that food must be imported, scarce foreign currency is required. Even in a developed country such as Japan, the sensitivity of the food import issue continues to have a profound effect on the Liberal Democratic Party's ability to retain power. When too many constituents perceive the United States to be placing undue pressure on Japan to liberalize its domestic agriculture markets, the repercussions can ripple across the entire trade economy as traders and consumers protest by becoming more conservative. This same pattern has played itself out in the past few years in South Korea, as well.

India may serve as an important model for agricultural and urban development in Greater Asia. Often overlooked, India is perhaps the most significant success story in Asia and the Pacific in this half-century as a relatively stable, secular, and multiethnic democratic polity. Famine has been virtually eliminated, partly because of the Green Revolution's remarkable impact as well as the fact that the country inherited from its former colonial overseers, the British, one of the most sophisticated transportation networks in Asia.

■ *Environmental pollution.* Large concentrations of people in urban areas produce many kinds of pollution. Industrial development and transportation require energy. Removal of human and industrial waste is mandatory. The costs of such environmental management may fall disproportionately on cities least able to pay for them. As a region, Asia may be distinguished by its urban population, but the majority of the rapidly growing cities found there, such as Manila, Jakarta, Bangkok, Seoul, Taipei, and Shanghai, are in developing or newly industrializing countries. China, for example, is extremely dependent on indigenous coal reserves to meet its economic development demands; at the same time, coal emissions in particular are now thought to contribute to global warming trends. Taiwan, significantly, has now admitted it has air, land, and water pollution problems so severe that it will require billions of dollars of expenditures during the next decade.

These problems are not limited to the nation-state. The prospect of global warming reminds us that the issue of environmental pollution does not begin and end at a given national boundary. As yet, no effective institutional models have been developed for solving the regional resource management problems confronting Asia. Whether the problem is managing fishing resources, disposing of toxic wastes, or improving air quality, the transnational nature of the problem demands international discussion and consensus, which is only now beginning to occur in the Pacific Basin and rimland countries. One important forum for discussion of the environment and other trans-Pacific matters was the 12-nation ministerial meeting on Asian Pacific Economic Cooperation in November 1989. Perhaps a portent of future developments in this area is that Australia and Japan—not the United States—have played leading roles in such discussions since the 1960s.

One conclusion regarding the challenges facing the urban centers of the Pacific Rim is that each contains both a local and a global component. At the global level, the most appropriate models for development need to be identified through comparative analysis. The challenges facing Asian cities probably cannot be met by relying simply on Western models, although the technology for addressing many environmental and infrastructure development needs may very well be found in the West (and in Japan).

At the local level, the obstacles to be overcome are even more difficult. Among these, local financing of infrastructure development looms large as one of the more difficult problems facing the developing countries of the Pacific. Many of these countries and cities have depended on outside assistance to meet capital needs. Perhaps in partnership with groups such as the Association for Investment Management and Research, alternative methods for freeing scarce local capital and for rewarding risk takers in the newly emerging service economy of these urban centers can be explored.

Conclusion

This presentation on the Pacific Rim and that of Alexander B. Murphy[1] on Europe emphasize the physical, economic, and cultural complexities of these regions. One fundamental difference, however, is that Asia has no overarching political structure for addressing regional development challenges.

City growth can be expected in each region. In Europe, relations (circulation) between city and hinterland will be reinforced as the Cold War ends, and Asian cities will continue to become major centers of fiscal concentration. The growth prospects in both regions include investments in transportation infrastructure, communication equipment, building materials, and environmental pollution control technology and related services, but local markets are as distinctive as the local geography (landscape) of each country. Thus, marketing approaches for each must differ.

Investors in both the Pacific Rim and Europe need to look beyond the nation-state as a category for organizing infor-

---

[1]Mr. Murphy's presentation begins on page 31.

mation about regional trends—as illustrated by the examples of substate (or trans-state) ethnic nationalism; the notion that communism is monolithic (everywhere the same), which it is not; or that Pacific Rim markets have universal characteristics.

We have entered a multipolar world in which the circulation of goods, services, and ideas will have a different pattern because of diverse centrifugal and centripetal forces. This pattern requires adaptation if firms are to compete. In a multipolar world, new issues such as resource distribution, population pressures, urban growth, and the need for new regional political/economical institutions take on greater importance. In assessing this bipolar world, investors should avoid conceptual blind alleys that result when making simplistic generalizations about the nation-state; transnational regional interaction may, in fact, be a far more significant indicator of the potential for long-term economic development, ethnic factionalism, and political stability.

Investing in the Pacific Basin

Andrew Economos
Principal
Scudder, Stevens & Clark

Important regional characteristics contribute to increased returns for investment portfolios in the rapidly expanding Pacific Basin. These include high levels of economic activity, increasing levels of foreign direct investment, rising living standards, and strong domestic demands.

The Pacific Basin is a diverse and broad region. Historically, the problem with investing there has been that investors, especially U.S. investors, tend to lump the region together and think of it as only Japan—too expensive, overvalued, and a place they do not understand. The area is diverse, however, and the society heterogeneous, encompassing different races, cultures, and sociopolitical environments. The wise investor is the one who looks at the particular parts of this region.

Pacific Basin Investment

Why invest in the Pacific Basin? Here are six of the many reasons:

■ *Stock market opportunities.* In the 1980s, the Pacific Basin accounted for 15 or 20 percent of the world's stock market capitalization, maybe even less; by 1991, the figure was 33 percent. So ignoring the area limits the investment opportunity set to Europe, which is friendly and familiar, Latin America, and the United States.

■ *Good returns.* Markets throughout the Pacific Basin, not just in Japan, have consistently outperformed most Western markets.

■ *High rates of economic growth.* The real reason for investing is to create true wealth. Some wealth creation elitism comes into play when looking at the Pacific Basin. U.S. and some European investors tend to think a German producing a BMW is more sophisticated wealth creation than the average Thai producing a Nike sneaker. Corporate profit growth rates are much stronger in Thailand, however, and we are able to take advantage of that. You should not associate ugly investing or ugly wealth creation with the Pacific Basin. Rather, it is a place that is growing dynamically and fairly consistently.

■ *Increasing regional prosperity.* Everyone in the Pacific Basin wants a second VCR and color television or a motorcycle instead of a bicycle. We are not just investing in the traditional multinational exporters, we are also investing in domestic demand—private consumption. As the Pacific Basin countries expand, their people begin to consume with a vengeance. The good Japanese citizen, for example, now is the one who consumes rather than the one who saves.

■ *Strong probusiness governments.* Having a government that is behind the economy—and ultimately the stock market—is a terrific combination for growth. During the 1970s and early 1980s, some of the Pacific Basin governments dabbled in centralized, socialist-type policies. As they looked at Japan, Taiwan, and Hong Kong, however, they began to realize that free market thinking and probusiness government development policies were the better tactics. As a result, the governments' attitudes have changed tremendously. They think of themselves as allies of business rather than the antagonists that we encounter in some other countries of the world.

■ *The Confucian ethic.* The Pacific Basin people respect authority, have a good work ethic, and emphasize education, which is critical in the long run. Their entrepreneurial spirit is probably unmatched anywhere in the world.

The dynamism of the Pacific Basin region is extremely critical. This area has complimentary comparative advantages within itself. It has industrialized countries such as Japan, which has capital and the latest technology. It also has the newly industrialized countries, which have the skills and middle management necessary to implement the policy and wealth creation from some of the more developed countries.

The number of opportunities in Asia is expanding. The region envelops India, the Philippines, Malaysia, Thailand, and China. The Indian market now includes Sri Lanka and Pakistan. The region also includes Vietnam, a high-growth economy now being unshackled from the communistic or socialistic system. Vietnam will undergo tremendous growth during the next decade. We are constantly amazed at the level of entrepreneurship in both the north and the south as the people are given their property back and are able to sell in a free market.

The Pacific Basin has distinct regional characteristics, and identifying them is important. Several of these contribute to increased or abnormal returns for our portfolio.

■ *High levels of economic activity.* A movement is afoot in the world toward regional trading blocs. Out of economic necessity, the Asians are starting to look into their own backyards for sources of raw materials and places to sell their goods.

■ *Increasing levels of foreign direct investment.* Many Pacific Basin countries are low-wage areas with ample raw materials and large labor pools. In their quest to eliminate low-value-added manufacturing at home, non-Asian companies are moving into the region to take advantage of these production advantages and to develop consumer markets there. The Japanese are extremely savvy about their approach to other Pacific Basin regions. Initially, they wanted only to access raw materials and large low-cost labor pools, but recently they came to realize that such a strong consumer market (180 million people in Indonesia alone) could offset any slowdowns in the rest of the world.

■ *Rising living standards and strong domestic demands.* Along with generally rising wages, growth in domestic demand is strong in the Pacific Basin countries. Not only is this area exporting and developing, it is also consuming a great deal, with the exception of Hong Kong, which has had a slowdown in its economy. Real wealth creation is taking place in the service and other domestic demand sectors.

Economic Growth

The Pacific Basin is a consistently high-growth area, even without Japan. With the exception of 1985, when the oil shock plunged the area into a recession, the economic growth gap between Organization for Economic Cooperation and Development countries and Asia has been consistent. In Japan or Korea, for example, people get depressed when economic growth goes from 13 percent to 8.5 percent a year.

Japan has had strong and consistent economic growth for at least a decade, and more of the Pacific Basin countries are looking to it as the region's engine of growth and to other Asian countries as sources of raw materials and destinations for their goods. These countries are rapidly shifting their export drives away from the United States and Europe and toward the rest of Asia. Two-way trade flows in the Pacific Basin amount to about $270 billion, and these flows are growing sharply each year.

The backdrop for all this growth has been very high savings rates. These savings supply the capital markets and also will help fund the expansion that will take place in these economies.

Foreign Direct Investment

The Pacific Basin countries have received huge waves of foreign direct investment. Australia, China, and

Indonesia have been the big beneficiaries. Between $1 billion and $2 billion a year of the foreign direct investment is going into these countries. Foreign direct investment has had a huge impact in the Pacific Basin. Almost without exception, some 2 percent of gross domestic product (GDP) can be attributed to this source. In some of the countries, such as Malaysia and Indonesia, it has contributed as much as 6 percent to GDP. The secondary ripple effect of foreign direct investment as it spreads through the region has had a tremendous impact on the region's economy.

The Japanese have been the big players in foreign direct investments. They like to describe the Pacific Basin as a great flight of geese with Japan at the front and the other countries taking up their positions behind it; foreign direct capital is moving backward through the flight of geese, again depending on comparative advantages and labor pools. The billions of dollars the Japanese have pumped into the region have not only provided raw materials and labor but newly developed consumer markets.

Wage Inflation

The newly industrialized countries are beginning to find themselves in the midst of wage inflation. As a result, they have had to increase the technological content of their goods. The only way they can do that is to push the low-value-added manufacturing into the rest of Asia as they try to diversify themselves and restructure their economies to take advantage of the changes in the 1990s. The Japanese are not the only big players in some of the smaller markets of Asia; Taiwan, Hong Kong, Korea, and Singapore have also been large foreign direct investors, again pushing out the low-value-added manufacturing as they try to find their niche in this particular area or in the global economy. Countries such as Korea and Taiwan have found themselves in a difficult position: They are positioned between Japan at the top with high technology and capital and, at the bottom, the lesser developed countries—a struggling but rapidly developing subregion that is trying to pursue and replicate the economic miracle of the newly industrialized countries.

Historically, capital has flowed from the developed economies to the newly industrialized countries, taking advantage of low wage rates and a skilled labor force. The second wave of capital flows is from the newly industrialized countries to the Association of South East Asian Nations (ASEAN) countries. Foreign direct investment is coming out of the ASEAN countries and moving into Vietnam, Sri Lanka, and Pakistan. The Thais are very active in developing Indochina, and the difference in wage rates shows the result. This area has very high productivity, so unit labor costs are rising. That is a concern for competitiveness. Vietnamese wages are between $15 and $20 a month, of which most goes to the government, so it is very competitive in wage costs.

Wages in the newly industrialized countries rose rapidly from 1986 to 1991, whereas wages in the ASEAN countries stayed relatively stable, growing about 23 percent in that particular region. About 60 percent of the population in Thailand and probably 80 percent in Vietnam and Indonesia work on farms. As soon as urban wage rates increase, rural people flood into the cities to seek the higher wage they are able to find in manufacturing. As a result, the potential labor force is large, which keeps a cap on wages.

Problems in the Pacific Basin

The transition to industrialization in the Pacific Basin is not likely to be without problems. Some of them are:

■ *Slower global trade.* These countries tend to be vulnerable and sensitive to changes in global trade. A slowdown, such as the global recession now in place, probably hurts them disproportionately. Regional exports from the Asian countries did slow down in 1990, but in 1991, the numbers picked up again, mainly because these countries have been increasing their slice of the market-share pie at the expense of the rest of the world, most notably the Europeans. As a result of their exports, they have been maintaining their wealth-creation position.

■ *Changes in industrial composition.* These countries are structurally in a transformation. The economies are moving from producing sneakers and garments to producing consumer electronics, automobiles, and other high-tech products. Many of these newly industrialized countries will push the low-value-added manufacturers into a captive labor force.

■ *Lack of infrastructure.* Many of the cities in these countries have poor telecommunications, sewage, and water infrastructure.

■ *Human resource development.* Many of these countries have a shortage of middle managers, accountants, engineers, and the other skilled people necessary to propel their economic growth away from low-value-added manufacturing to the higher skilled pursuits. The problem is compounded by higher wage rates in manufacturing as compared to academia. Experienced teachers, who should be training the next generation of engineers, are lured from academia into the marketplace. In losing their stock of academics, these countries will not be able to train the next generation of middle mangers.

■ *Emphasis on the financial markets.* Historically, Asia has used debt capital to grow, but these countries are starting to realize they must use their equity markets. As a result, the Asian equity markets have grown in market capitalization, not only from stock price appreciation but also from new initial public offerings. One of the interesting points about Asia is that in many of these countries, the best companies have yet to come into the markets because they are tightly held by business families. These companies have no incentive to open up their books to the tax authorities. The governments realize this, and they are starting to propose development policies that encourage and stimulate the private sector with tax incentives and other gimmicks.

Intra-Asia Trade

Intra-Asia trade is developing as these countries look inward. Some 50 percent of the region's trade either originates or has its final destination in Asian markets. This is important in sustaining the region as the rest of the world starts to reject some Asian exports.

Many of these countries, Hong Kong and Taiwan, for example, are developing captive labor forces for their particular goods or their multinationals' goods. The special economic zones in China are a huge labor force approximately 60 million strong for Hong Kong manufacturing. Hong Kong manufacturers also have some 6 million workers in the special economic zones for their operations, compared with about 1 million workers in Hong Kong working for Hong Kong manufacturers. What happens to these workers in 1997 is going to be very critical for Hong Kong.

Other countries are looking for opportunities as well. Thailand is looking to the rest of Indochina for its source of raw materials and is also seeking to open up the golden triangle markets for Thai goods. In addition, the Thais think of themselves as the financial services center for the Indochina peninsula.

Singapore and Malaysia are taking advantage of low wages in some of the underdeveloped areas of Malaysia and also in some of the places in Indonesia where the huge labor force in the agrarian sector is untapped. Singapore is beginning to use its goods, services, technologies, skills, and capital to develop certain targeted industries that will compensate for its shortage of manpower.

A tremendous amount of synergy is possible when the two Koreas unite. South Korea has capital and technology, and North Korea has raw materials and a large labor force. Some of the multinational Koreans are currently circumventing the government and talking directly with the North Korean government. The change will be facilitated by economic necessity rather than by political change. South Korea has some pilot manufacturing programs in operation in several areas around China with large populations of Korean-speaking Chinese.

Infrastructure Investments

The Pacific Basin has a tremendous shortage of infrastructure. All you have to do is get stuck in a Bangkok traffic jam to realize why cellular communication is growing so strongly in the area. The Japanese are leading the way in infrastructure development. Japan has the per capita gross national product necessary to make $3.3 trillion of such improvements during the next 10 years, which comes out to about $1 billion a day spent on infrastructure. Some huge projects are in the works. Also, Japan will have the ability to stimulate its economy when things start to slow down. Taiwan has $310 billion to spend on infrastructure, and even South Korea plans to spend about $160 billion during the next five years.

In most Pacific Basin portfolios, the managers have liberally included infrastructure-related stocks—cement companies, building materials, civil engineering firms, and the like. These investors will be beneficiaries of this trend as it takes place. In the longer term, infrastructure stocks could be an opportunity for outside investors.

Education is a real problem in Pacific Basin countries. Literacy is fairly high in Asia, but at a sixth- or seventh-grade level. High school or secondary education is also fairly strong. The real shortage is university-level education. Some of the smaller countries of Asia lack university-educated students, and that is going to be a problem. Many of the students see no point in deferring high wages while they earn an accounting or engineering degree when they can make money now by going into the private sector.

Financial Markets in the Pacific Basin

As stated earlier, Asia accounts for a big part of the world's stock market opportunities. From 1984 to 1990, the U.S. market grew about 130 percent, European markets about 400 percent, and Asian markets about 600 percent. This growth has come from price appreciation and also from many new company listings, which expand the investment opportunity set.

Among the individual countries, Indonesia is a real outlier—about 7,000 percent growth in market capitalization. That market went from 12 stocks, of which 4 or 5 were eligible for foreign investment, to about 192 stocks. The markets in South Korea, Thailand, and Taiwan grew more than 1,000 percent each in market capitalization. The punters are beginning to realize they can make money in the stock market, and the companies and their managers are beginning to realize that they can use equity financing to overcome the high cost of capital in the world.

Asia is a high-volatility market, as measured by standard deviation of return, but investors are being compensated by a higher return. In addition, this region still provides diversification benefits for U.S. investors. Singapore and Malaysia, which have about a 50 percent correlation with the Standard & Poor's 500, are the exceptions. Correlations with the U.S. market are statistically insignificant in all the other markets. Some correlations are very low. For example, during the market crash of 1987, the Korean stock market moved to a new high. Most of these markets are dancing to the tune played by their own economies. The Asian countries also differ in their cycles and positions in the global economic cycle.

Conclusion

Our business has become way too quantitative. We try to slice and dice alphas and betas, and we compare price–earning ratios across the range. Investors are beginning to forget that they are investing in people and ideas. Without those, assets do not mean much. This is very important to remember when looking at Asia. These people have entrepreneurial spirit. Given the right stimulus by government and the world economic community, they take charge of their lives and take off economically.

Asia is famous for many of its sayings. One that sprang up in the Special Economic Zones illustrates what is happening in the region and the mind-set of these people: "When you see a green light, you must drive very, very fast. When you see a red light, you must find another road." That is exactly how the Chinese are looking at the region. They are going around all the government obstacles, all the socialism in the way, and they are taking advantage of the situations that present themselves.

Currency Management

Michael R. Rosenberg
Manager of International Fixed-Income Research
Merrill Lynch & Co.

Because conventional asset allocation separates the bond decision from the currency decision, bond managers typically look at relative absolute total return performance. The optimal approach, however, considers excess returns, in which currency managers overweight the currency offering the highest yield-adjusted return.

The best-performing markets, whether bond markets or equity markets, are not always associated with the best-performing currencies. Thus, separation of the currency and investment decisions makes sense. Most investment managers who manage global bond portfolios recognize that the currency decision must be separate from the market decision.

Separation of Currency and Bond Market Decisions

Optimally allocating a portfolio for market exposure and currency exposure requires two unique decisions. First, the global bond manager should overweight those bond markets that will offer the greatest incremental performance to the portfolio as a whole, which seems intuitive. Second, the currency manager should overweight the currencies that are expected to provide the greatest incremental performance to the portfolio as a whole. What may seem intuitively correct, however, is not necessarily optimal in practice.

Investment managers have three alternatives for separating currency and bond market exposures. A manager with a large staff can maintain a separate unit to manage only the currency exposure of a portfolio and another unit to manage only the market exposure of that portfolio. That would be an ideal separation. A manager with a small staff usually centralizes these decisions into one small unit that manages both the market and the currency exposures. A manager who is not confident in managing the currency exposure can farm out the management of the currency risk to a currency overlay manager and manage only the market risk internally.

An international fund manager—either an equity or a bond manager—has a wider set of investment choices than a U.S. domestic fund manager. For example, assume an international bond manager operates in a two-country world, consisting of the United States and Germany. The manager has four investment choices, which are shown as a matrix in **Figure 1**. If the manager wants to overweight U.S. dollars, he can either own U.S. bonds outright—therefore having dollar exposure—or he can own deutsche mark bonds hedged into dollars. To overweight deutsche marks, he can own deutsche mark bonds outright or own U.S. bonds hedged into deutsche marks. To overweight U.S. bonds, he can either own U.S. bonds outright or own U.S. bonds hedged into deutsche marks. Similarly, to overweight deutsche mark bonds, he can either own deutsche mark bonds outright or own deutsche mark bonds hedged into dollars. Only one of the cells in that matrix will provide the optimal total return for this two-country world.

Sometimes, what may seem intu-

Figure 1. Currency/Bond Market Decision Matrix

	Currency Decision	
	Overweight Dollars	Overweight Deutsche Marks
Overweight U.S. Bonds	Own U.S. Bonds Outright	Own U.S. Bonds Hedged into Deutsche Marks
Overweight DM Bonds	Own DM Bonds Hedged into Dollars	Own DM Bonds Outright

(Row label: Bond Market Decision)

itively correct actually results in the wrong investment decision. This point can be illustrated in the case in which the currency decision is separated from the bond decision. Assume that the bond manager chooses which bond market to overweight and the currency manager decides which currency to overweight. Take, for example, the situation shown in **Table 1**, which shows projected returns for the German and U.S. markets. German bonds are projected to return 10 percent in deutsche mark terms during the coming year. The money market return, the cash return on German assets, is expected to yield 9 percent in deutsche marks. In the United States, the projected return on bonds is assumed to be 8 percent in U.S. dollar terms, and the money market return is 5 percent. Table 1 also shows that Germany's short-term rates are 4 percent higher than U.S. short-term rates. This means the dollar will trade in the forward exchange market at a premium of 4 percent or that the deutsche mark will trade at a discount of 4 percent. Because U.S. short-term rates are lower than German rates, the market expects the dollar will rise over time against the deutsche mark by 4 percent.

Intuitively, a bond manager would think the German market superior to the U.S. market. Because the German market's absolute returns are higher, overweighting German bonds would seem to make sense. As shown in **Figure 2**, however, the optimal allocation should be to overweight the U.S. market, not the German market.

Suppose the currency manager chooses to overweight U.S. dollars. If the bond manager hands the currency manager U.S. bonds, he leaves the currency exposure unchanged because U.S. bonds, being dollar denominated, earn 8 percent. If the bond manager hands the currency manager German bonds, which are expected to offer a 10 percent return, the currency manager has to hedge the deutsche mark risk associated with those German bonds by selling the deutsche mark forward in the foreign exchange market. Because the cost of selling deutsche marks forward is 4 percent, the return on the hedged German bonds is only 6 percent. So the optimal decision if the manager wants to overweight dollars is to overweight U.S. bonds, even though U.S. bonds offer a lower absolute return than German bonds.

Now suppose the currency manager wants to overweight deutsche marks. The best strategy once again is to overweight U.S. bonds. If the bond manager hands the currency manager German bonds, which offer a return of 10 percent, the currency manager does not need to hedge the deutsche mark risk, because he wants to be long deutsche marks. If the bond manager hands the currency manager U.S. bonds, he must hedge the dollar risk by selling dollars forward into deutsche marks at a premium of 4 percent. Through hedging, the total return on the hedged U.S. bond position is 12 percent.

Table 1. Bond Market Decision—Absolute vs. Excess Returns

Item	Germany		United States	
Bond return	$R_G^{DM} = 10\%$		$R_{US}^{\$} = 8\%$	
Cash return	$r_G^{DM} = 9\%$		$r_{US}^{\$} = 5\%$	
Excess return	$R_G^{DM} - r_G^{DM} = 1\%$	$R_{US}^{\$} - r_{US}^{\$} = 3\%$		
Short-term interest rate differential	$r_G^{DM} - r_{US}^{\$} = 4\%$	$FP_\$ = FD_{DM} = 4\%$		

Figure 2. Currency/Bond Market Decision Matrix—U.S. /German Example

	Overweight Dollars	Overweight Deutsche Marks
Overweight U.S. Bonds	$R_{US} = 8\%$	$R_{US} + FP_\$ = 8\% + 4\% = 12\%$
Overweight DM Bonds	$R_G + FD_{DM} = 10\% - 4\% = 6\%$	$R_G = 10\%$

Clearly, this example shows that the market that offers the highest absolute return is not necessarily the market an investor should overweight.

Market Selection

Excess return is the key to selecting the market that will offer the highest return for a global bond portfolio. The market to overweight is not the one that offers the highest absolute return but the market that offers the greatest excess return relative to cash.

Figure 3 illustrates this proposition. At the outset, we assume that the U.S. money market return is 5 percent, the U.S. bond return is 8 percent, the German money market return is 9 percent, and the German bond return is 10 percent. The United States has a steeper total return curve than Germany's total return curve. The steeper U.S. total return curve permits the creation of synthetic securities out of these U.S. bonds, denominated in other currencies, that offer a superior return. As Figure 3 shows, the return curve for U.S. bonds hedged into deutsche marks is parallel to, but 4 percentage points higher than, the U.S. bond curve. By taking this steeper total return curve from the United States, embedding it in deutsche mark space, we find that U.S. bonds hedged into deutsche marks will provide a superior return to German bonds.

Suppose the manager is interested in overweighting deutsche marks because he thinks the deutsche mark offers the best long-term appreciation potential. Under the circumstances assumed in the example, U.S. bonds hedged into deutsche marks offer superior total return performance relative to owning

deutsche mark bonds outright. If the manager thinks the dollar is the currency of choice, even though he believes German bonds will provide higher absolute total return, buying German bonds and hedging them into U.S. dollars will not produce a better total return than buying U.S. bonds outright, even though the German bonds offer a higher overall absolute return.

Figure 3. Projected Total Return Analysis, Domestic vs. Currency-Hedged Foreign Bonds

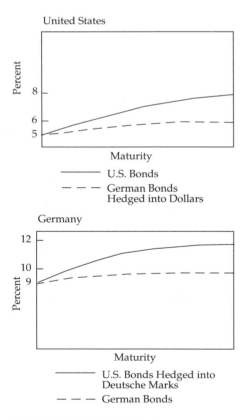

United States

U.S. Bonds
German Bonds Hedged into Dollars

Germany

U.S. Bonds Hedged into Deutsche Marks
German Bonds

Importance of the Yield Curves

Yield curves and their shapes can have a major bearing on whether an investor should be owning foreign bonds outright or U.S. bonds hedged into foreign currency, or vice versa. The slope of the U.S. yield curve today is highly positive. Short-term rates are about 4 percent, and long-term rates are about 8 percent. Germany has the exact opposite situation—an inverted curve. Short-term rates in Germany today are about 9.5 percent, and long-term rates are 8 percent. Although long-term rates in Germany and the United States are roughly the same, the two short-term markets are quite different—by about 550 basis points.

The slopes of the U.S. and German curves offer two interesting opportunities for a fund manager who might want to own deutsche mark bonds. He can buy U.S. bonds hedged into deutsche marks or buy deutsche mark bonds outright. Given the current yield curves, he could buy a U.S. bond at 8 percent and sell the dollar forward at a premium of 5.5 percent, which equals the short-term interest rate differential. This creates a synthetic deutsche-mark-denominated security on a three- or six-month rolling basis yielding about 13.5 percent today—the 8 percent U.S. bond return on top of the 5.5 percent premium earned by selling the dollar forward into deutsche marks. Buying the German bond outright earns only an 8 percent return during the three- or six-month holding period.

The story does not end here, however. Because the United States has a positively sloped yield curve, if U.S. and German yields remain unchanged, holding a bond over a 3-, 6-, or 12-month period permits the investor to roll down the U.S. curve over time. If the investor buys a five-year bond and holds it for one year and it rolls down to a four-year bond in one year's time, he is able to generate capital gains on the roll down the yield curve. If he buys a five-year German bond, however, he rolls up an upwardly sloping German yield curve, generating capital losses. Factoring in the capital gain on a U.S. bond hedged into deutsche marks as the investor rolls down the curve, and considering the capital loss that rolling up the German yield curve generates, the spread between hedged U.S. bonds and German bonds is even more substantial. The total return difference could be about 700 basis points in an unchanged yield curve environment.

The outcome would be different, of course, if a tremendous rally occurs in the German bond market relative to the U.S. bond market. The rally would have to be on the order of 175 basis points during the coming year, however, for five-year German bonds to match the yield and total return pickup from owning U.S. bonds hedged into deutsche marks.

In the early 1980s, this situation was entirely reversed. The United States had an inverted yield curve and Germany had a positively sloped curve. At that point, an investor could create synthetic dollar-denominated securities by buying German bonds hedged into U.S. dollars as an alternative to owning U.S. bonds outright, providing strong total return pickups over the U.S. bond market outright.

Currency Management

Yield is an important consideration in currency decisions, as it is in bond management. Too often, currency managers ignore yield, or the income that can be earned, on a net currency position. A lot of currency managers like to trade in and out, trying to catch the short-term trends in currencies, and sometimes taking positions based on a one-day or two-day time horizon; a week is the long-term view for many currency managers. Ignoring the income that could be earned on a net currency position can lead a currency manager to make incorrect portfolio bets. As **Table 2** shows, currency managers should place more emphasis on yield-adjusted currency returns and focus less on the short-run change in the currency itself.

Table 2 compares two scenarios. In Case 1, the deutsche mark is expected to weaken by 2 percent against the dollar; in Case 2, the deutsche mark is expected to weaken by 5 percent. Assume that the U.S. cash return is once again 5 percent,

Table 2. Currency Decision, Absolute vs. Excess Return

Item	Case 1	Case 2
Expected percent change in DM [$E(DM)$]	–2%	–5%
U.S. cash return ($r_{US}^{\$}$)	5	5
German cash return (r_{G}^{DM})	9	9
$r_{G}^{DM} - r_{US}^{\$}$	4	4
Projected excess return: $[E(DM)] + (r_{G}^{DM} - r_{US}^{\$})$	+2	–1

and the German cash return is 9 percent—a 4 percentage point differential. If a currency manager is short-run oriented and the deutsche mark begins to weaken, he may immediately short the deutsche mark and go long the dollar. If it only weakens by 2 percent over a 12-month horizon, however, he is better off being long deutsche marks because he can earn a 4 percent higher money market return compared to a U.S. money market investment. The excess return on being long deutsche marks is 2 percent after accounting for the 2 percent currency loss. Had the deutsche mark weakened by 5 percent, and had the currency manager stayed long deutsche marks during that period, even the large 4 percent yield pickup would not have been enough to compensate for the currency loss, and he would have had a net loss of 1 percent. The important point is that yield can provide an important cushion.

In today's world, European money market rates are 600 basis points higher than U.S. money market rates, a significant cushion should the dollar strengthen during the next year. If the dollar is expected to rise by 6 percentage points from current levels, an investor would be indifferent between owning European or U.S. money market investments. The only way a manager would want to be long dollars in today's world is if he thinks the dollar will rise by more than the 6 percent yield differential Europe offers. If he thinks the dollar may go higher, but not by a full 6 percent, he should overweight the European currencies.

Table 2 shows that, too often, a currency manager ignores the money market yield pickup and shorts the deutsche

mark. He would be right to short the deutsche mark if it weakens significantly, but he may end up with inferior returns if the deutsche mark only weakens a little. He may be right that the deutsche mark weakens, but he can still lose in terms of asset allocation. This problem is illustrated in **Figure 4**. In both cases, the expected cash return in Germany is 9 percent. In Case 1, the deutsche mark is expected to weaken by

Figure 4. Projected Return on Alternative Cash Investments in U.S. Dollar Terms

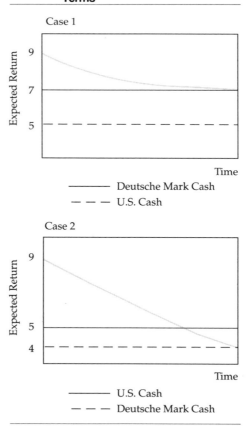

Case 1

Deutsche Mark Cash
U.S. Cash

Case 2

U.S. Cash
Deutsche Mark Cash

2 percent, leaving a 7 percent return at the end of the period. The expected return in the United States is 5 percent, so under a scenario in which the deutsche mark is expected to weaken only slightly, the investor is better off being in German cash. If the deutsche mark is expected to weaken a lot, however, as in Case 2, he is better off owning U.S. cash during that period. What matters is the yield pickup plus the expected change in the currency. If the manager is confident that the deutsche mark will weaken, but not necessarily by a lot, then he must factor in the yield pickup that German assets offer in determining the net currency allocation.

Conclusion

In the conventional approach to asset allocation, in which the bond decision is separated from the currency decision, a bond manager typically only looks at relative absolute total return performance—in the example used here, the absolute performance of German bonds compared to that of U.S. bonds. Whatever the difference is in the two markets, the bond manager typically weights the market that provides the highest absolute performance. Many currency managers look at the short-run change in the currency and often ignore the income that can be earned on that currency position.

The optimal approach should consider excess returns. The bond manager's decision should be based on the expected bond market return relative to the money market return in each market, overweighting the market with the highest excess return. The currency manager's decision should be to overweight the currency offering the highest yield-adjusted return—in other words, the change in the currency plus the income that can be earned on that currency position.

The Forgotten Side of Global Investing—Trading and Custody

Richard A. Kos, CFA
Vice President, Director of Client Service
Frank Russell Securities, Inc.

Trading cost and turnover have a negative effect on portfolio performance. Although turnover is decreasing throughout the world, trading costs remain high outside the United States.

Trading and custody costs are important considerations in global investing. Plan sponsors, fund owners, and institutional investors are very aware of the tactical and strategic goals of managing their total transaction costs, which include commissions, market impact costs, and opportunity costs. As practitioners, however, less is known about the magnitude and variability of these costs across the major global markets.

This presentation summarizes the results of an empirical analysis of the global transactions of Russell clients from 1987 through the third quarter of 1991. The universe characteristics are shown in **Table 1.** The analysis focused on the explicit components of trading costs—commissions and taxes. The implicit trading costs attributable to market impact were not considered. All transactions and portfolios from Russell's U.S. and multicurrency Portfolio Verification System (PVS) were used in the analysis. Portfolios were not excluded or screened to approximate a representative universe.

Trading cost calculations were performed at the transaction level, and turnover and portfolio impact calculations were performed at the portfolio level, with median results reported to mitigate most of the "noise" associated with the statistical outliers. Trading costs are defined as explicit transaction costs expressed as a percent of the transaction amount. Turnover is calculated in the traditional manner and represents the lesser of total purchase or sale transaction amounts divided by the average market value of the portfolio for the period. Portfolio impact of trading costs is defined as the total trading costs for all transactions expressed as a percent of the average market value of the portfolio. This represents the level of performance "lost" because of trading costs.

Trading Costs

Trading costs vary greatly from country to country and region to region. **Figure 1** shows the average trading costs, broken down by commissions and taxes by region. Among the regions, North America is the cheapest and Europe the most expensive in which to trade.

Within these regions, as **Figure 2** shows, the United States is the cheapest market to transact in at 15 basis points, and the United Kingdom is the most expensive at 44 basis points. The cost of trading in the United Kingdom was higher than expected. Through the first three quarters of 1991, commission costs were 24 basis points and taxes were 20 basis points. The taxes represent the average taxes paid during the year, so in a market like the United Kingdom, which has a purchase-only stamp duty of 50 basis points, the average depends on whether more securities are bought or sold in a particular period. If purchases

60

Table 1. Universe Characteristics, 1987–91

Year	Number of Countries	Total Principal ($US billions)	Number of Trades	Number of Portfolios
1987	28	$170	410,006	3,200
1988	29	92	421,030	3,400
1989	32	125	449,033	4,000
1990	33	110	486,057	4,200
YTD (3Q91)	36	118	447,471	5,400

Source: Frank Russell Securities' Portfolio Verification System.

equal sales during the period, the taxes would be 25 basis points.

Japan is the second highest cost market, with transaction costs of 38 basis points. The average commission cost of 29 basis points was not a surprise, but the 9 basis points for taxes and fees was lower than expected. This may be explained by the fact that the transaction tax in Japan is applied only to sales transactions.

The transaction costs in Germany are similar to those in Japan, with an average cost of 36 basis points—33 basis points in commissions and 3 basis points in taxes. The cost of trading in Canada is 28 basis points.

Trading Cost Trends

Because trading costs change over time, we studied trends in trading costs during the past five years. Figures 3 through 7 show the average trading costs, turnover, and portfolio impact of trading costs for portfolios in the United States, Japan, United Kingdom, Canada,

and Germany from 1987 through 1991.

Commissions and taxes in the United States have been trendless since 1987 at about 15 basis points. This is significant because, within recent history, this is the first time any type of cost leveling has occurred in the United States. Since 1975, when U.S. commission rates were deregulated, commission rates have been in a free fall, dropping roughly 70 percent from their 1975 levels. In fact, anecdotal evidence suggests that had volume not recovered in 1991, the rates would probably have gone up for the first time in 15 years. During the 1987–90 period, turnover and the portfolio impact of trading costs in the United States generally declined (**Figure 3**).

What is the significance of these statistics at the portfolio level? If investors know what they are paying each time they go through the gate (i.e., trading costs), and they know how many times they go through the gate (i.e., turnover), then they know what is lost in performance results because of trading costs.

Figure 1. Global Trading Costs, Regional Comparisons, 1991

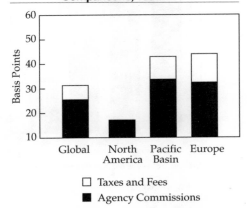

□ Taxes and Fees
■ Agency Commissions

Source: Frank Russell Securities' Portfolio Verification System.

Figure 2. Global Trading Costs, Five Largest Markets, 1991

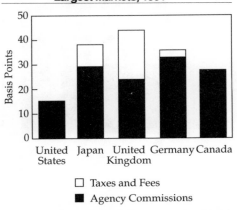

□ Taxes and Fees
■ Agency Commissions

Source: Frank Russell Securities' Portfolio Verification System.

Figure 3. Trading Trends—United States

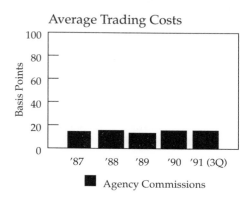

Average Trading Costs

■ Agency Commissions

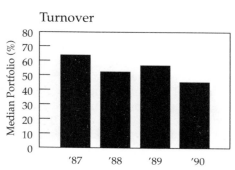

Turnover

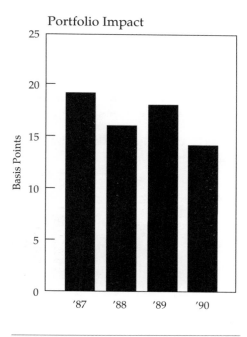

Portfolio Impact

Source: Frank Russell Securities' Portfolio Verification System.

Figure 4. Trading Trends—Japan

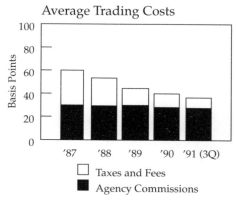

Average Trading Costs

□ Taxes and Fees
■ Agency Commissions

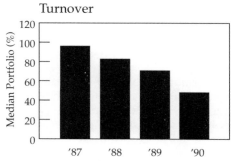

Turnover

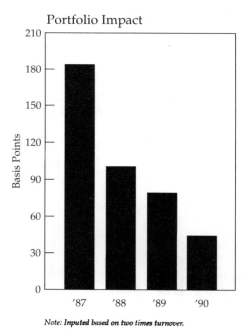

Portfolio Impact

Note: *Imputed based on two times turnover.*

Source: Frank Russell Securities' Portfolio Verification System.

In 1990, if an investment manager could have traded at zero cost, his performance would have been 14 basis points higher at the median portfolio, a very low number relative to most research published on this subject.

In Japan, trading costs, turnover, and the portfolio impact of trading costs have all been decreasing since 1987 (**Figure 4**). This trend reflects several factors, including the state of the market, the entry of non-Japanese managers who have a longer investment horizon and lower turnover, and a movement toward passive management.

The trend in average trading costs since 1987 is basically flat in the United Kingdom (**Figure 5**) and Canada (**Figure 6**), similar to the situation in the United States. Turnover is coming down in both markets. As a result, the performance lost to trading costs is less. Germany has experienced some decrease in average trading costs since 1987 (**Figure 7**). This decline in rates may, in part, reflect Germany's attempt to regain some of the market share it lost to London. With turnover basically static since 1988, the portfolio impact of trading costs bounces around within a fairly tight range.

Commission Variability

The variability of commission rates is also of interest. **Figure 8** shows statistics on commission rate variability for the five major markets in 1991. In general, commissions varied widely across the universe of players. Because larger deals generally have lower commission costs, the average is lower than the median in some countries. Some of the variability is explained by the pricing structure. For example, in a market that prices on a cents-per-share basis, the basis point cost will vary with the price of the share. The same 6-cent commission on a $20 stock generates twice the commission rate in basis points as it would on a $40 stock. This explanation applies to the United States and Canada.

Another explanation may be based on investment managers' familiarity with pricing norms in each of these markets. For example, a review of Russell's U.S. transactions revealed that invest-

Figure 5. Trading Trends—United Kingdom

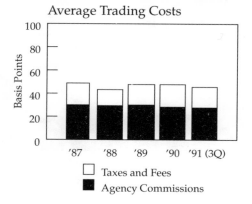

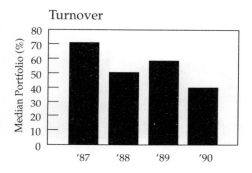

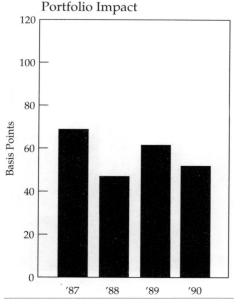

Source: Frank Russell Securities' Portfolio Verification System.

ment managers domiciled outside the United States were paying 38 basis points when they traded in the United

Figure 6. Trading Trends—Canada

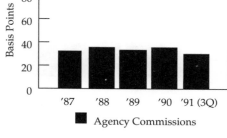

Average Trading Costs

■ Agency Commissions

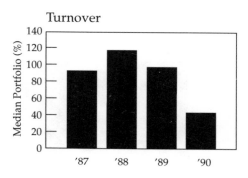

Turnover

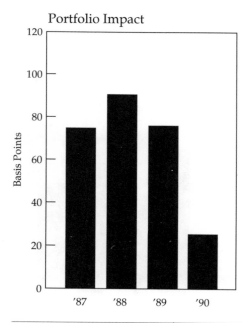

Portfolio Impact

Source: Frank Russell Securities' Portfolio Verification System.

Figure 7. Trading Trends—Germany

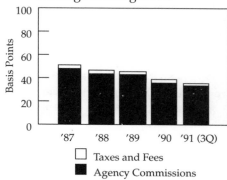

Average Trading Costs

☐ Taxes and Fees
■ Agency Commissions

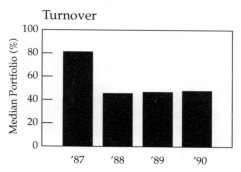

Turnover

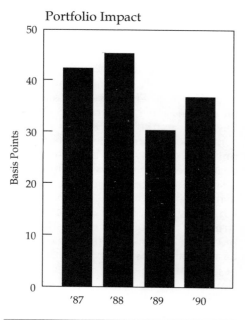

Portfolio Impact

Source: Frank Russell Securities' Portfolio Verification System.

Figure 8. Commission Rate Variability, 1991

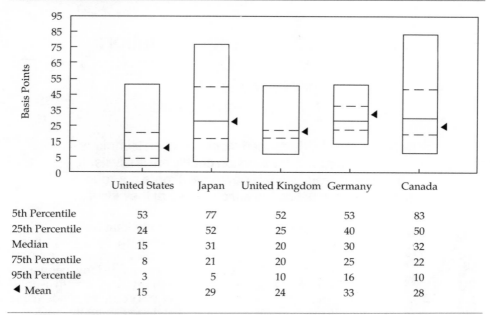

	United States	Japan	United Kingdom	Germany	Canada
5th Percentile	53	77	52	53	83
25th Percentile	24	52	25	40	50
Median	15	31	20	30	32
75th Percentile	8	21	20	25	22
95th Percentile	3	5	10	16	10
◀ Mean	15	29	24	33	28

Source: Frank Russell Securities' Portfolio Verification System.

States, between two and three times the rate being paid by their counterparts domiciled in the United States. Not surprisingly, 38 basis points is very close to the rate levels considered "normal" in two of the regions outside North America. Apparently, they were paying up when they did not need to, assuming that rates in the U.S. market approximated the rates paid in their local markets.

The variability in U.S. rates also can be explained by the "jostling" for market share between the traditional first-tier firms, which are trying to increase agency commission rates, and the various crossing networks and off-exchange alternatives, which are competing on price at 2 or 3 cents a share. As a result, costs are widely dispersed around the mean as the two forces compete. Meanwhile, the average simply plods along, creating a false sense of tranquility.

Conclusion

Trading costs are changing around the world. The U.S. market is far and away the cheapest market to trade equities in, and the trend line has been flat during the past five years. If anything, costs may be under some upward pressure. Outside the United States, explicit trading costs are higher, but they are declining. Turnover is decreasing throughout the world. Turnover is not a problem if an investor can earn excess returns, but all other things being equal on the performance front, low turnover is preferred to high.

The negative impact of trading costs on portfolios is high outside the United States. Although the impact is generally declining, higher costs still represent some very real hurdle rates for investment managers to beat in reaching the mythical land of alpha.

Advances in Equity Valuation

Jason MacQueen
Chief Executive Officer
QUANTEC Investment Technology Ltd.

**Because any clearly defined stock selection technique
can be tested with information coefficient analysis,
investment professionals now have a more rigorous
method for evaluating the effectiveness of their ideas.**

Novice fund managers quickly learn several reliable methods of systematically outperforming the market, such as buying low price–earnings ratio (P/E) or high-yield stocks. Only much later in their careers are they initiated into the more arcane mysteries of fund management, such as the reasons few fund managers actually follow their own stated beliefs.

Investment mythology assumes that faith alone will be a sufficient defense of these beliefs. Today, however, managers can use investment technology to test such ideas more rigorously. In particular, any clearly defined stock selection methodology can be tested with information coefficient analysis.

Advances in Modeling

During the past 10 years, quantitative techniques have become more widely accepted in the investment community. More analysts are taking an interest in building their own models rather than buying them. For a long time, the name of the game has been persuading people that "You need a model; buy ours." This was part of the grand strategy of selling people quantitative approaches as they would a religion: You have to have faith in the models. For example, even if one religiously used an optimization technique to identify the efficient frontier, to demonstrate that doing so actually added value to the investment process would take a very long time.

One problem with many quantitative models is that they depend on accurate forecasts of returns. Many people assume that the models are easy to use and that the forecasts could be made using the historical data. Generally, however, the quality of "historic" forecasts has not been good.

Quantitative models have been used for about 10 years in Europe. People are now much more familiar with optimizers. They have generally accepted the idea of using rigorous, systematic, disciplined investment approaches as opposed to traditional seat-of-the-pants management. They also have elevated their understanding of these processes to the point that they can criticize them. For example, managers on both sides of the Atlantic now recognize that quadratic optimization is too sensitive to small changes in the input and it requires precise point forecasts of return, among other problems.

As people have become more familiar with the idea of optimization, they have begun asking more detailed questions about the process. Two or three years ago, people began focusing on generating the return forecasts that go into the optimization process. Europeans are showing growing interest in developing systematic models—for stock selection or equity market forecasting, for example.

Equity valuation modeling can be divided into two types: quantitative and qualitative, which includes traditional, subjective, and seat-of-the-pants management. Quantitative forms of equity valuation modeling can be divided into linear models and nonlinear models. Mathematically inclined analysts have a fascination with nonlinear models. About every five years, some incredibly complex piece of mathematics is introduced as *the way* to forecast the market. The most recent one is chaos theory. Five years ago, it was catastrophe theory. People claimed that catastrophe theory could be used to predict when the market was suddenly going to fall or when some stock was suddenly going to take a nosedive. Needless to say, after about a year of excitement, articles, and promises, catastrophe theory sank without a trace. Models based on chaos theory will probably fade as well.

Linear models may be single-factor or multifactor models. This distinction is slightly artificial, because single-factor models are, after all, only special versions of multifactor models. Examples of single-factor models include market models, the low price–earnings tilt model, and the small-capitalization tilt model. The point of the distinction is to focus attention on the construction of multifactor models, which should provide greater stability—and hence better long-term performance—than any single-factor model could.

Multifactor model inputs may be microeconomic data (individual stock characteristics), macroeconomic variables, or both. Of course, arbitrage pricing theory uses neither type. It uses pure factor analysis on returns data to construct the "best possible fit" multifactor model. Unfortunately, clear identification of the factors is usually impossible, and the stability of the factors (or even the number of factors) is not guaranteed over time.

Testing Stock Selection Methodologies

Several issues must be considered when testing stock selection methodologies, including the definitions and methodological variations used in the model, whether the model is based on facts or forecasts, whether it uses a projectable economic rationale or is simply data mining, the range of the model's validity, its range of applicability, whether the data are ranked or raw, the shape of the distribution, when the model works, and what it means to say a methodology "works." The low-P/E example will illustrate these points.

■ *Definitions and methodologies.* Understanding the definitions and methodologies used in the model is important. Having a low P/E is fine, but it is not significant until you know how it was calculated. Is it an actual P/E, a prospective P/E, or a relative P/E? If it is relative, it could be relative to the stock's history, the market, the industry, or a dozen variations, all of which are P/Es and all of which might warrant testing. Do not think about only one definition of P/E, because better variations may be possible.

■ *Fact based or forecast based.* Another very important consideration is whether the methodology is based on facts or forecasts. A trailing P/E— today's price divided by the last known earnings—is a fact-based methodology. Today's price divided by a forecast of next year's earnings is a forecast-based methodology. A P/E is fact based if it is based on information widely known throughout the market, such as a consensus earnings forecast. Individual analyst's forecasts of earnings, which are presumably unknown to the market at large, are forecast based. Fact-based methodologies generally do not perform as well as (perfect) forecast-based ones. Prospective P/Es nearly always outperform trailing P/Es. Fact-based methodologies are easier to apply, however, because they need only historical data.

■ *Projectable economic rationale or data mining.* The most important thing to guard against in stock selection is data mining or, in other words, finding relationships in a set of data that are entirely accidental and therefore nonsystematic. Out-of-sample testing is one way to avoid this. Another more intellectual way is to develop a projectable economic rationale for the methodology that will be tested before the testing process begins. For example, before testing whether a factor is related to high returns, some reason exists to believe it will generate high returns. If instead the test is based solely on the apparent correlation, no grounds exist for believing the relationship will continue working in the future.

■ *Range of validity.* The range of validity relates to the range of values allowable in the model. **Figure 1** illustrates a typical relationship between P/Es and returns. The ideal relationship is that within the oval area. Lower P/E stocks are associated with high returns, higher P/E stocks with low returns, and average P/E stocks with average returns.

In making these hypotheses, however, the linear effect across the range of possible values of what is being defined is important to consider. A low-P/E effect is usually present in most major Anglo–Saxon markets for most stocks with P/Es with sensible values. A high-P/E effect, in which stocks with very high P/Es do well, is also present. One reason is that some high-P/E, low-earnings stocks are on their way up, having just recovered from a bad period. Another group of high-P/E stocks are high-growth stocks, those with rapidly growing earnings at very high multiples. These companies are likely to continue to grow fast and provide high returns for some time. These high-P/E stocks cloud the issue if they are included in backtests.

Another problem with accepting the

"low P/E is good, high P/E is bad" philosophy is the negative-P/E stocks. These stocks clearly have a low P/E, but they are also losing money and are probably going down the tubes. Clearly, these stocks should not be considered low-P/E stocks for the purpose of selecting a portfolio. For other strategies, deciding where the boundary lies is much more difficult. Sometimes testing is the only way to establish a good boundary. If all of the data points are included, the results will be much weaker and the information coefficient will be lower. In fact, the results may be so weak that if the analyst has not looked at the whole picture, but just at some numbers, he may be tempted to discard the model as useless.

■ *Range of applicability.* Another consideration is the range of applicability, or the range of stocks for which the methodology will work. For example, the price–book-value ratio is not equally applicable to all stocks. On an *ex post* basis, it might be a good indicator for industrial stocks, but usually it does not have any value and it certainly does not mean the same thing for financial stocks (whose assets are largely financial rather than plant and machines).

■ *Ranked or raw data.* This decision relates to the issue of how fine the discriminatory power of the model is. How far apart must two values be to be meaningfully different? The actual number may not have any information content; for example, P/Es of 7.6 and 7.7 are not meaningfully different. Often, only the ranking in the universe is important. If all of the stocks in a universe have very high P/Es—as in Japan—then the mean actual value will be different from the mean actual value in the U.S. or U.K. market. In general, however, "lower" P/E stocks will tend to outperform "higher" P/E stocks, even though "low" and "high" mean different things in different markets.

■ *Shape of the distribution.* The shape of the data distribution—normal, linear, fat-tailed, or one-sided, for example—is also an important consideration. The type of data—that is, raw or ranked—and the shape of the distribution are related. If ranked data are used

Figure 1. Range of Validity, Low-P/E Model

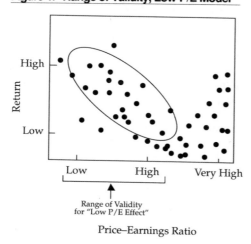

to smooth the distribution, how should they be ranked? Several schemes are possible. A universe ranking of 500 stocks, for example, would involve a ranking from 1 to 500. Alternatively, the stocks could be grouped, perhaps into deciles or quintiles. The grouping could be equally weighted or normally weighted. Unfortunately, grouping destroys some potentially useful information. A normal distribution could be used to identify the outliers of the distribution, which would occur only in the top and bottom groups. That process may have some merit, but it destroys the information in the distribution of the underlying data. Another possibility, known as interval ranking, is to rank the data so as to preserve their underlying distribution and preserve the information that may be in it. Suppose the range of validity for P/Es for U.S. stocks is from 2 to 20. All stocks with P/Es between 2 and 4 would be designated rank 1; those between 4 and 6, rank 2; and so on. The shape of the ranked distribution will then correspond very closely to that of the actual underlying data, and any information inherent in the shape of the distribution will not be lost by the ranking process.

■ *When the model works.* The next step is to determine when the process works. Models do not always work. During some long periods, the model may work, and sometimes the process works better than other times; at other times, it may not work at all. For example, during some periods, high-P/E stocks tend to outperform low-P/E stocks.

■ *Defining what works.* To say "low P/E works" is to assert the existence of a P/E factor in which the premium, or factor return, is negative. The contribution of this factor to any stock's return is equal to the P/E factor premium multiplied by the stock-specific factor coefficient—by the P/E of the stock. Note that a low P/E times a negative P/E factor premium gives a low negative contribution to the stock's return; all other things being equal, this will result in the stock's return being higher than average.

Factor Premium Models

Discovering that low P/E works most of the time immediately raises the question of why the P/E factor premium varies in size and sign. With a model of the factor premium, a multifactor stock-selection model with dynamic weights for the factors could be constructed. Factor premiums are usually modeled with the same kinds of macroeconomic variables, such as GNP growth or interest rate changes, that would be used to model the market's returns.

Figure 2 illustrates the general form of a multifactor stock selection model based on microeconomic inputs. Each factor contributes to the stock's return.

Figure 2. Bottom-Up Modeling

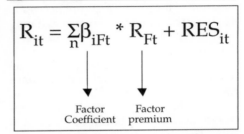

$$R_{it} = \sum_n \beta_{iFt} * R_{Ft} + RES_{it}$$

Factor Coefficient   Factor premium

Source: QUANTEC Investment Technology Ltd.

There are k factors, and each factor's contribution to the return on the stock consists of two pieces—the factor coefficient and the factor return (or factor premium). **Figure 3** shows the form of a multifactor model of the market returns, using a number of macroeconomic variables.

Suppose a multifactor model for stock selection is based on a number of

Figure 3. Top-Down Modeling

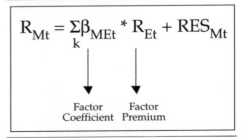

$$R_{Mt} = \sum_k \beta_{MEt} * R_{Et} + RES_{Mt}$$

Factor Coefficient   Factor Premium

Source: QUANTEC Investment Technology Ltd.

microeconomic variables, such as P/Es, yields, small caps, high caps, earnings momentum, and price momentum. In this formulation, the factor coefficients are given. The problem is to determine the factor returns, or factor premiums. If the assumption is that low P/E works, and some P/Es for a universe of stocks are given, then the procedure is to attempt to prove that the P/E factor premium is negative. A low P/E times a negative factor return will produce a small negative contribution to the return on the stock. This would be better than a stock with a high P/E times a negative factor return, which is going to give a large negative contribution to the return on the stock.

Thus, the assertion "low P/E works" means that the P/E factor premium is negative. This premium is not necessarily stable through time, however. It may fluctuate in size and will even reverse itself from time to time. The problem is this: After initially testing the model using historical P/Es, what determines the size and sign of the P/E factor premium? The P/E factor itself is a macroeconomic variable, but not of the usual sort. The conventional macroeconomic variables—inflation, interest rates, GDP growth, oil prices—can, however, be used to explain the P/E factor premium. This problem's formulation is given in **Figure 4**, in which the R_{Ft} are the factor premiums.

The formulation of the problem is basically the same, but some macroeconomic variables are added. Changes in GDP, inflation expectations, and other macroeconomic variables are important. Then a slightly different problem arises: to discover the sensitivity of the P/E premium to each of the macroeconomic variables. In most cases, these

Figure 4. Dynamic Coefficients for Bottom-Up Models

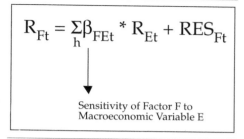

$$R_{Ft} = \sum_h \beta_{FEt} * R_{Et} + RES_{Ft}$$

Sensitivity of Factor F to Macroeconomic Variable E

Source: QUANTEC Investment Technology Ltd.

macroeconomic variables do not need to be forecasted. A lagged relationship may work. A fall in interest rates, for example, may take some time to filter through to stock earnings and affect the stock's performance.

Conclusion

People who think they are building models using stock-specific information, such as P/Es, yields, earnings growth, and earnings momentum are making assumptions about market factors. These factors are not necessarily macroeconomic factors in the traditional sense, but they are likely to be simply combinations of normal macroeconomic variables.

Historically, model builders have perceived themselves as being in one of two camps: those who base their model building on individual stock characteristics, and those who use a top-down approach, building models based on macroeconomic variables. Both approaches are really aspects of the same problem: How can they be combined to construct a multifactor model with dynamic weights?

Advances in Equity Valuation Models

Peter Muller
Manager, Valuation Services
BARRA[1]

Building valuation models has become an acceptable pursuit for both scholars and practitioners. Four approaches to equity security valuation dominate: value, momentum, low volatility, and links to macroeconomic variables. Hot topics include quadratic optimization and futures/swaps.

Until recently, the gospel of market efficiency ruled finance academia. Papers documenting exploitable inefficiencies were not accepted for publication. Only practitioners openly claimed the possibility of skill in outperforming market benchmarks. The gospel has changed.

In this presentation, I will address some broad issues involving how valuation ideas evolve. A few hot topics in quantitative finance related to active portfolio management also will be discussed.

Both traditional analysis and quantitative models may be used in valuation. Traditional analysis values one asset, or company, at a time. Although traditional analysts use some quantitative tools, they rely largely on research, company visits, and storytelling.

A typical story might be: "PETCUTZ is a new company that provides haircuts for pets. There are about 100 million pets in this country. Assuming two haircuts a year at $10 a cut, this is a $2 billion business. Say you only get 10 percent—that is $200 million. Current revenues are $500,000, which means there is a potential for PETCUTZ to increase by 400 times its current size. The stock is cheap at 4 times projected revenues."

In contrast to traditional analysis, the quantitative approach uses computers to analyze many assets simultaneously. Each stock is compared to every other stock in the market. Such inputs as past financial statement data, consensus growth estimates (from traditional analysts), and past stock price behavior are used in a multivariate valuation model. In the end, the quantitative analyst also tells stories (you will hear some soon) focusing on why certain strategies do or do not work.

Figure 1 illustrates the quantitative modeling process. The quantitative manager uses computers, models, back-tests, and judgment to process data from multiple sources and derive a relative valuation model. The more data are available, the easier it is to build a historical model, but this is not the goal. Only predictive models are of value. As data availability increases, discretion and judgment become increasingly important aspects of the model-building process.

Basic Quantitative Approaches

Two basic quantitative approaches to relative valuation are value and momentum. Based on company fundamentals, the value approach assumes that at a given time, every stock has a fair price, or at least a fair price relative to other stocks. Over time, stocks are assumed to move toward their fair price; therefore, stocks that are undervalued relative to

[1]Mr. Muller now is a vice president at Morgan Stanley & Co., Inc.

Figure 1. The Quantitative Management Process

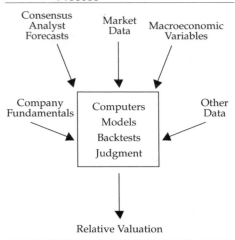

Consensus Analyst Forecasts — Market Data — Macroeconomic Variables

Company Fundamentals — Computers Models Backtests Judgment — Other Data

Relative Valuation

Source: BARRA.

their fair price are desirable, and stocks that are overvalued relative to their fair price are not. The difficult aspect of a value approach (of course!) is determining how various stock attributes, such as book value, dividend yield, revenues, earnings, and projected growth, determine this fair price. In addition, patience is required because stocks are as likely to move away from their fair price as they are to move toward it (for example, bank stocks in late 1990). Finally, shocks affecting a company or its industry can quickly change the fair price, which means managers are shooting at a moving target. Simple value models rank companies based on price–earnings or price–book ratios. Slightly more complicated models include dividend discount models and free cash flow models that estimate a stock's value as a multiple of estimated future free cash flow.

Momentum models use a different approach. The idea behind momentum models is that investors are slow to react to good news, causing stocks that have been doing well relative to the market to continue outperforming. The simplest momentum models rank stocks only on price performance (relative strength) and are grouped under technical analysis. Other types of momentum models examine historical growth of earnings or revenues, or alternatively, trends in analysts' earnings estimates.

Figure 2 and **Figure 3** show the performance of value and momentum factors, respectively, in five major equity markets during the past eight years. In most cases, the value factor is based on an earnings–price ratio, and the momentum factor is based on relative strength. The lines on each graph represent the cumulative multiple factor return to a bet on the value or momentum factors in each market. Multiple factor returns are neutral to the market, industry factors, company size, and other identifiable market factors. The returns shown in Figures 2 and 3 are from BARRA's multiple factor models in each country. These models were not built to find exploitable anomalies but rather to characterize stocks by factors predicting volatility. Using some of these factors in valuation has been an unexpected benefit.

Both value and momentum factors are important determinants of asset returns in all five markets. Notice that the performance of both value and momentum factors was generally positive during the 1984–91 period. In many cases, the mean monthly return to these factors was greater than zero with 95 percent statistical significance.

Figure 2. Performance of Value Factors in Different Markets, December 1983–December 1991

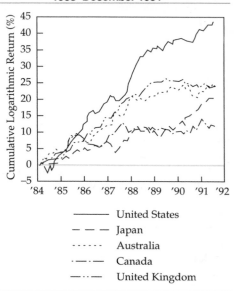

United States

Japan

Australia

Canada

United Kingdom

Source: BARRA.

Caution is necessary, however. Although value has worked exceptionally well in the current Japanese bear market, the recent performance of value factors in some other markets has not been strong. Momentum strategies have worked especially well in Canada and Australia, but a strong relationship between momentum and liquidity in both markets makes implementation potentially difficult.

Maintaining a healthy skepticism with regard to valuation models is important. Practitioners desiring to use quantitative valuation models should consider that well-known strategies may not continue to work in the future. Nevertheless, risk-controlled value and momentum strategies (when properly implemented) will probably continue to add a small amount of positive incremental return.

Links Between Macroeconomic Data and Stock Returns

Another popular school of quantitative model building attempts to exploit the relationship between macroeconomic data and asset returns. Practitioners use such variables as interest rates, inflation, industrial production, and exchange rates to help outperform equity benchmarks.

Imagine looking ahead one month to the values of selected macroeconomic variables. Could this information be used to help an investment manager beat the market during the next month? During the 1973–89 period, BARRA built a model linking residual asset returns[2] to the following macroeconomic variables: short- and long-interest rates, inflation (as measured by changes in the Consumer Price Index), bond credit spreads, industrial production, exchange rates (dollar–yen and dollar–deutsche mark), unemployment, and oil and gold prices. The model was built assuming perfect knowledge of the next month's macroeconomic variables. Then, the correlation between predicted and realized residual asset returns during January 1990 was examined. January 1990 data were added to the model, and returns were predicted for February 1990, and so on, through December 1991.[3]

Table 1 presents the correlation between expected and actual residual returns over the approximately 1,300 stocks in the BARRA high-capitalization stock universe (this correlation is sometimes referred to as an information coefficient). The results indicate that with knowledge of next month's macroeconomic data, an equity benchmark can be outperformed. For 1990 and 1991, 22 of the 24 correlations are positive, and 15 of 24 are positive and significantly different from zero at the 95 percent level. As Table 1 shows, the average correlations are 0.15 for 1990 and 0.12 for 1991. Although predicting macroeconomic data is difficult, accurate macroeconomic predictions can be used successfully to predict asset returns.

Some practitioners have recently been successful using current macroeco-

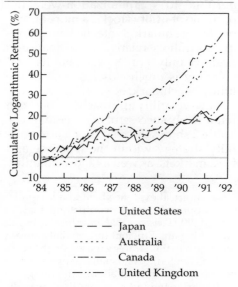

Figure 3. Performance of Momentum Factors in Different Markets, December 1983–December 1991

—— United States
– – – Japan
· · · · · · Australia
· —· — Canada
—· · — United Kingdom

Source: BARRA.

---

[2]Returns are defined as residual to the BARRA high-capitalization stock universe. By using residual returns, relationships between the macroeconomic variables and total market return are excluded.

[3]For more details on this simulation, see "Macroeconomics and Active Management: Is There a Connection?" *BARRA Newsletter* 140 (January/February 1992):21–25.

Table 1. Simulation Results—Monthly Information Coefficients, 1990 and 1991

Month	1991	1990
January	0.41	0.20
February	0.17	0.12
March	0.20	0.16
April	0.10	0.05
May	0.01	−0.06
June	0.04	0.05
July	0.03	0.26
August	0.12	0.30
September	0.11	0.15
October	−0.05	0.35
November	0.00	0.09
December	0.25	0.18
Average	0.12	0.15

Source: BARRA.

Note: Correlations equal to or greater than 0.08 are significant at the 95 percent level.

nomic data to predict future asset returns.[4] This approach is easier to implement because it does not require predictions of macroeconomic variables.

Low-Volatility Strategies

Low-volatility strategies have generated considerable interest in recent years. The basic idea behind these strategies is that portfolios with lower volatility will generate returns equal to or greater than portfolios with higher volatility. The theoretical justification behind a low-volatility approach is not nearly as compelling as that behind the capital asset pricing model (CAPM). Empirical evidence for the past two decades, however, has strongly supported a low-volatility approach, while empirical support for the theoretically opposed CAPM during the same period has been limited.

Low-volatility strategies are attractive for several reasons. First, historically, they have worked incredibly well in different markets during different time periods. Second, low-volatility strategies incorporate a nonlinear dynamic. Not only do these strategies tend to buy stocks with low betas and low residual volatility but they also focus on portfolios with component assets having low correlations with one another. Third, unlike most other nonlinear ideas, building a minimum-variance portfolio is relatively easy.

Any active U.S. equity manager would have been happy with the results of a low-volatility approach during the 1970s and 1980s. **Figure 4** graphs the annual performance of a low-volatility strategy relative to the S&P 500 for the 1973–90 period. The y-axis shows active portfolio return (portfolio return minus S&P 500 return), while the x-axis shows relative risk (portfolio volatility minus S&P 500 volatility). The low-volatility portfolios were created at the beginning of each year by finding the fully invested portfolio of U.S. equities with minimum variance.

Each data point represents one year of data. Note that 15 of the 18 data points fall in the desirable northwest quadrant, indicating that a low-volatility portfolio outperformed the S&P 500 with less risk. In the other three years, the portfolio had lower volatility but underperformed.[5]

Figure 5 attempts to put this result in context, comparing the low-volatility portfolio to a capitalization-weighted portfolio of utility stocks, a more appropriate benchmark. Note the low-volatility portfolio's relative performance is negative only 3 of 18 years, but its total volatility is much closer to that of the utility benchmark.

Low-volatility approaches have been remarkably successful in other markets. **Table 2** shows the results of a low-volatility strategy within the Japanese and U.K. markets, as well as a low-volatility

---

[4]See, for example, Robert D. Arnott, "Forecasting Factor Returns: An Intriguing Possibility," *Improving Portfolio Performance with Quantitative Models* (Charlottesville, Va.: Association for Investment Management and Research, 1989), pp. 25–32.

[5]The empirical evidence behind a low-volatility approach was so compelling that, in early 1990, *Pensions and Investments* began publishing an "Efficient Index" that showed the return to this strategy (based on the work of Bob Haugen). As usually happens when people get too excited about something, the first quarter the index went "live" was the worst quarter ever experienced.

Figure 4. Efficient Index—Risk and Return Relative to S&P 500, 1973–90

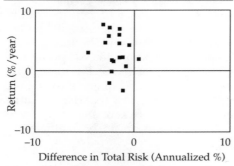

Source: BARRA.

Figure 5. Efficient Index—Risk and Return Relative to Cap-Weighted Utility Portfolio, Rolling Five-Year Periods, 1978–90

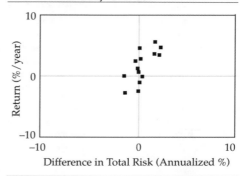

Source: BARRA.

asset allocation strategy designed to beat the Europe/Australia/Far East Index (EAFE). Minimum-variance, fully invested portfolios were created quarterly, and their subsequent performance was compared to a benchmark. For the EAFE case, asset weights within country portfolios were fixed, and only country weights were allowed to change. For each example, the low-volatility strategy had a higher return and lower risk than the respective benchmark.

The Bigger Picture

Not every manager can beat the market, but some do. Where do great investment ideas come from, and how do they evolve? Thus far, four approaches to active management used by successful quantitative managers have been described: value, momentum, macroeconomic links, and low volatility. These approaches are reasonably well known and hence will probably not exhibit ex-

traordinary performance in the future. As Bill Sharpe once wrote, "Good investment ideas carry within themselves the seeds of their own destruction." The more people who are familiar with an approach, or the more easily an approach can be identified in data, the worse it will work.

Thus, evolution and agility, not size and stability, are desirable qualities in an investment manager. Twenty years ago, the first purely quantitative equity managers built stable processes that worked for a long period of time. Then they lost effectiveness when others started copying them (and beating them at their own game). Today, a top quantitative manager needs a process that is dynamic and changes quickly.

Several practices can help active managers in this regard:

■ Start listening to new ideas early.

Table 2. International Low-Volatility Strategies

Market	Time Period	Benchmark Return[a]	Benchmark Risk	Low-Volatility Portfolio Return[a]	Low-Volatility Portfolio Risk
Japan (TSE1)	1980–91	10.26%	18.44%	11.31%	15.08%
United Kingdom (FTA)	1983–91	8.40	18.76	11.00	12.70
International (EAFE)	1988–91	8.44	17.43	20.99	16.98

Source: BARRA.

Note: All return and risk numbers are annualized and expressed in percentage terms.

[a]Japanese and U.K. returns are excess to the risk-free rate. International returns are total returns to U.S. investors.

Market inefficiencies come and go, so managers should build an internal research process to constantly test and monitor strategies and be the first to exploit opportunities.

■ Reduce the required comfort level. If managers require their strategies to backtest successfully over 15 years, they will be less likely to find a strategy that works in the future.

■ Think in terms of shorter time spans and evolving strategies.

Hot Topics in Implementation

Up to this point, different approaches to valuation have been discussed. Active managers should also think about how valuation models are turned into portfolios. With this in mind, let me address four hot topics in implementation.

■ *Is there a better way than quadratic optimization to construct a portfolio?* No. Recent research has shown that for a given set of expected returns, optimizers build portfolios that are more efficient *ex post* than other methods.[6]

■ *Should I consider using short sales in my active portfolio?* Yes. Active managers have insights about whether stocks are overvalued or undervalued. A long-only portfolio can take a very limited bet against overvalued stocks. Under most circumstances, allowing for short positions enables a manager to achieve better risk-adjusted return relative to a benchmark.

■ *Is there a better way to measure risk than variance?* No, with exceptions. In theory, semivariance or downside risk better characterizes undesirable portfolio performance, but for most equity portfolios with close to symmetrical returns, variance and semivariance are indistinguishable. Estimating downside risk also is much more complicated than estimating variance, and estimation error will more than offset the advantages of using a more precise measure.

■ *Should I consider using futures and/or swaps to manage a portfolio?* Yes. Recently, a number of pension funds have outperformed the S&P 500 by indexing to the Nikkei 225 and getting 200–300 basis points for swapping the Nikkei return for the S&P return. This opportunity may no longer be available, but others are sure to arise. Counterparty credit risk in many of these swaps still appears to be inefficiently priced.

Conclusion

Given the limited format and reasonably broad scope of this presentation, many subtleties necessary to make effective use of momentum, value, macroeconomic links, and low-volatility techniques have not been addressed.[7] Each strategy provides an opportunity to add value, but value is by no means a sure thing. Value and momentum have worked reasonably well in the past, but most quantitative practitioners are familiar with these approaches. Macroeconomic links help predict asset returns, but macroeconomic information is difficult to predict accurately. Low-volatility strategies have worked extremely well historically, but they are less likely to work as well in the future.

The successful quantitative manager of the 1990s will be familiar with these approaches but will be constantly looking for new ways to add value. Flexibility is important. Allow for evolution (revolution) in the investment management process. Abandon the comfort of a 15-year backtest and be willing to try new strategies reasonably quickly if they make sense and appear to work. Build a strong internal research process. Look for good ideas, and quickly implement them.

Finally, consider alternative ways of implementation. Allowing short sales can increase a strategy's value. The growing swaps/derivatives market can

[6]For more details, see Peter Muller, "Empirical Tests of Quadratic Optimization," Proceedings of the Wharton Conference on Financial Optimization (London: Tims, Forthcoming 1992).

[7]For a more in-depth article on the use of different quantitative factors in equity valuation, see Bruce I. Jacobs and Kenneth N. Levy, "Disentangling Equity Return Regularities: New Insights and Investment Opportunities," *Financial Analysts Journal* (May/June 1988):18–43.

also provide opportunities. Every possible advantage is important. Even with better data and faster computers (or maybe because of them), there is little doubt that the active management game is getting tougher.

Order Form₀₁₃

Additional copies of *Investing Worldwide III* (and other AIMR publications listed on page 79) are available for purchase. The price is **$20 each in U.S. dollars**. Simply complete this form and return it via mail or fax to:

AIMR
Publications Sales Department
P.O. Box 7947
Charlottesville, Va. 22906
Telephone: 804/980-3647
Fax: 804/977-0350

Name _____

Company _____

Address _____

_____Suite/Floor _____

City _____

State _____ZIP _____ Country _____

Daytime Telephone _____

Title of Publication	Price	Qty.	Total
_____	_____	_____	_____
_____	_____	_____	_____

Shipping/Handling
- ❑ All U.S. orders: Included in price of book
- ❑ Air mail, Canada and Mexico: $5 per book
- ❑ Surface mail, Canada and Mexico: $3 per book
- ❑ Air mail, all other countries: $8 per book
- ❑ Surface mail, all other countries: $6 per book

Discounts
- ❑ Students, professors, university libraries: 25%
- ❑ CFA candidates (ID #_____):   25%
- ❑ Retired members (ID #_____):   25%
- ❑ Volume orders (50+ books of same title): 40%

Discount $-_____

4.5% sales tax
(Virginia residents) $_____

7% GST
(Canada residents,
#124134602) $_____

Shipping/handling $_____

Total cost of order $_____

❑ Check or money order enclosed payable to **AIMR**   ❑ Invoice me

Charge to: ❑ VISA   ❑ MASTERCARD   ❑ AMERICAN EXPRESS

Card Number:_____   ❑ Corporate ❑ Personal

Signature:_____ Expiration date: _____

Selected AIMR Publications*

The Financial Services Industry—Banks, Thrifts, Insurance
  Companies, and Securities Firms, 1992 . . . . $20

Managing Asset/Liability Portfolios, 1992 . . . . $20

Investing for the Long Term, 1992 . . . . $20

A New Method for Valuing Treasury Bond Futures Options, 1992 . . $20
  Ehud I. Ronn and Robert R. Bliss, Jr.

Ethics in the Investment Profession: A Survey, 1992 . . . . $20
  E. Theodore Veit, CFA, and Michael R. Murphy, CFA

The Transportation Industry—Airlines, Trucking, and Railroads, 1992 $20

Earnings Forecasts and Share Price Reversals, 1992 . . . . $20
  Werner F.M. De Bondt

The CFA Study Guide, 1993 (Level I, Level II, or Level III) . . . . $20 each

Corporate Bond Rating Drift: An Examination of Credit
  Quality Rating Changes Over Time, 1991 . . . . $20
  Edward I. Altman and Duen Li Kao

Investing Worldwide II (1991), Investing Worldwide (1990) . . . . . . $20 each

Managing the Investment Firm, 1991 . . . . $20
  James R. Vertin, CFA, Editor

The Founders of Modern Finance: Their Prize-winning
  Concepts and 1990 Nobel Lectures, 1991 . . . . $20

The Poison Pill Anti-takeover Defense: The Price of Strategic
  Deterrence, 1991 . . . . $20
  Robert F. Bruner

Performance Reporting for Investment Managers: Applying the
  AIMR Performance Presentation Standards, 1991 . . . . $20

Initiating and Managing a Global Investment Program, 1991 . . . . . $20
  William G. Droms, CFA, Editor

Understanding Securitized Investments and Their Use in
  Portfolio Management, 1991 . . . . $20
  Ken M. Eades, Diana R. Harrington, and Robert S. Harris, Editors

Analyzing Investment Opportunities in Distressed and
  Bankrupt Companies, 1991 . . . . $20
  Thomas A. Bowman, CFA, Editor

Program Trading and Systematic Risk, 1990 . . . . $20
  A.J. Senchack Jr. and John D. Martin

*A full catalog of publications is available from AIMR, P.O. Box 7947, Charlottesville, Va. 22906;
804/980-3647; fax 804/977-0350.